RECALLING
THE SCOTTISH COVENANTS

RECALLING
THE
SCOTTISH COVENANTS

HUGH WATT

Professor of Church History, New College,
Edinburgh University

THOMAS NELSON AND SONS LIMITED
LONDON EDINBURGH PARIS MELBOURNE
TORONTO AND NEW YORK

First published May 1946

TO MY WIFE

FOREWORD

No period of Scottish history has proved more pregnant with far-reaching results than the Age of the Covenants. The English-speaking world of to-day still bears the impress in thought and institution of the contests of the two Scottish generations from the 1630's to the 1690's. The great questions at issue will constantly be re-examined by all who are interested in the development of political and ecclesiastical theory ; the loyalties and sacrifices displayed by leaders and common folk will continually attract all who are drawn to the heroic elements in the spirit of man. Phases of the protracted struggle will long be debated as they have been in the past ; episodes in which one side or the other soiled the standard under which it professed to fight will continue to confuse the issue ; the excesses committed by both parties in the heat of the struggle or on the seat of power will be set over against each other ; Dunaverty will be confronted with Dunottar, Philiphaugh with Rullion Green, as in the controversies of yesterday. Echoes of the conflict will persist so long as the party system, and the party mind, prevails among men.

This little volume is not an attempt to rewrite the history of a great movement. The names of many noted leaders are absent from its pages. Nothing is said of the divisions of the Commonwealth, nor of those most significant years when, under the second Charles, the Covenants were repudiated and burned and their adherents subjected to every known form of suppression.

Its origin and make-up can be simply explained. Its
contents have been largely determined by the incidence
of dates. During the last ten years commemoration
has been made in Scotland of the critical events of
three hundred years ago, and there have been some
celebrations, though greatly curtailed by the war. On
the central occasions, recalling events from 1636 to
1643, it has been laid upon me either to write or to
speak. Four of the papers which follow were thus
called forth. Their length was determined by the
commission. But the work for these papers raised
certain other questions which kept demanding an
answer. To these I devoted close attention, and found
opportunity for presenting, in select gatherings, the
conclusions I had reached. Of two of the six papers
I was able to obtain off-prints ; of other two, copies
of the periodicals in which they appeared. So constant
has been the demand for these, particularly from overseas, than it can no longer be supplied, and it was
suggested to me that they ought to be gathered and
published. With this suggestion I resolved to comply.
The determining reason was that, while some of the
papers survey familiar fields, two, at least, raise questions new to most, and help to shed light on imperfectly
surveyed areas of our Scottish religious history.

My thanks are due to the editor of *Life and Work*
for permission to reprint the first paper, and to the
editor of the *Scotsman* for similar permission for the
second and fifth papers. The fourth paper has already
appeared in an abbreviated form, but supplied with
full references, in the *Transactions of the Scottish Church
History Society*, Vol. vii, Part 3. The third and sixth
papers are printed here for the first time.

I desire to acknowledge the valued services of Miss E. R. Leslie, M.A., B.Com., assistant librarian at New College, and Rev. Thomas Maxwell, B.D., secretary of the Scottish Church History Society, the former in the preparation of the manuscript, and the latter in the reading of the proofs.

H. W.

NEW COLLEGE, *August* 1945

CONTENTS

RECALLING
THE SCOTTISH COVENANTS

FIRST PAPER

THE CANONS OF 1636

THREE hundred years ago this month [1] there appeared from the printing press in Aberdeen a tiny volume of forty-three pages which was to prove the prelude to the covenanting struggle. Its title-page ran, 'Canons and Constitutions Ecclesiasticall, Gathered and put in forme, for the Governament of the Church of Scotland. Ratified and approved by His Majesties Royall Warrand, and ordered to be observed by the Clergie, and all others whom they concerne. Published by Authoritie. Aberdene, Imprinted by Edward Raban, dwelling upon the Market-Place, at the Armes of the Citie, 1636. With Royall Priviledge.' The Canons had obtained the royal warrant in the preceding May, though, having been altered after that date, the printed form had to receive a renewed authorization, as appears from a letter from the Earl of Stirling to Maxwell, Bishop of Ross. There was considerable doubt in responsible quarters in London as to the warmth of their reception north of the Tweed. Juxon, Bishop of London, declared in a letter acknowledging receipt of his copy, that ' perchance at first [they] will make more noise than all the cannons in Edinburgh Castle ;

[1] Published in June 1936

I

but when men's ears have been used awhile to the sound of them, they will not startle so much at it, as now at first.' They did make a great deal of noise. John Row's indictment in thirty-five heads at the end of his history is a weighty bombardment. But it was soon forgotten when the heavier artillery came into action over the matter of the Liturgy.

THE HISTORY OF THE CANONS

It had been markedly evident since the Glasgow Assembly of 1610 and the institution of the Episcopate that the earlier Books of Discipline were out of date. While the Presbyterian structure of the Second Book of Discipline still functioned, at least as regards Kirk-sessions and Presbyteries, there had been introduced with the Episcopate an element foreign to that book, and indeed antagonistic to its fundamental principle. The leaders of the new era felt the need of new standards. The Assembly of 1616 had given instruction that a Book of Canons be prepared ' drawn forth of the books of former Assemblies, and where the same is defective, that it be supplied by the canons of councils and ecclesiastical convocations of former time.' It had even appointed a committee of two to put them into form. Whether the two ever completed their work or not is doubtful ; it is not certain that they even began it.

On their visit to Scotland, Charles and Laud had noted this glaring lack of any constitution in harmony with what the Church was, or with what they hoped it would become ; and it seems that Laud himself, in consultation with some of the younger Scottish bishops,

2

set about remedying this deficiency. But there was no search for precedents among the Acts of former Assemblies. To Laud the natural course was to take the latest Canons of the Church of England—the Constitutions and Canons Ecclesiastical of 1604—and to bring these into closer harmony with his ideal of a Church. A great part of the Scottish book is a verbatim transcript of the English one. It is through the failure to recognize this that some modern assessments are wide of the mark. They read into canons drafted to meet the English situation in 1604 and the conflict with the Puritans, explicit references to the Scotland of 1636.

That the few Scottish bishops taken into consultation were, in this matter, merely the executive officers of the King and his Archbishop is evident from this. Six months after the book had received the royal sanction Laud heard that Bellenden, Bishop of Aberdeen, had allowed a fast to be kept in his diocese on a Sunday. The King, he wrote to the Scottish Primate, had been very much displeased, and he adds, ' His Majesty's will and pleasure is, that if the Canons be not already printed, as I presume they are not, that you make a canon expressly against this unworthy custom, and see it printed with the rest.' Hence Chapter XIV, with this definite prescription, 'Neither shall it be lawful to keep, or indict, any Fast upon Sundays ; but only upon week-days, and such as shall be appointed by His Majesty.' Thus it appears, as we might expect, that the King's main adviser was Laud.

The Contents of the Canons

In view of their origin—drawn up in England and based on English models—it is natural that one main source of offence should be their omissions. The Presbyterian courts had vanished. Ruling elders were ignored. In chapters where we might expect them mentioned, we find instead, more than once, church-wardens, and once the ' six chief men of the Parish,' closely following 1604. The deacons of the Second Book of Discipline had disappeared, instead there were deacons after the Anglican model. The Church of Scotland was no longer to be an Episcopacy super-imposed on Presbyterianism, it was to be an Episcopacy pure and simple.

In regard to their positive prescriptions, the Canons departed from those of 1604 in the direction of a stronger emphasis on the Sacraments. Fears were expressed that the rules for ordination came near to reviving Orders as a Sacrament, that the regulations for confession and absolution with the seal of secrecy were not far removed from Auricular Confession, and that the directions relating to the Lord's Supper implied a drawing nearer to the doctrine of Transubstantiation, despite the fact that the adoration of the bread is explicitly condemned. But these were not the most ominous features. In the book itself it was felt that there were two special points of menace. It contained a prohibition not only of extemporary prayer, but even of the discretionary ritual of Knox's Liturgy. Divine service was to be done according to the Book of Common Prayer, before all sermons. Those who asserted that the form of worship therein prescribed contained anything repugnant to the Scriptures were to be excommunicated. And no-one had seen the proposed Book of Common Prayer, nor was it in their hands till more than another year had passed !

The other ominous feature was its uncompromising assertion of the King's supremacy in Church matters. The final right of appeal lay to him ; and those who impeached, in any part, his royal supremacy in causes ecclesiastical were to be excommunicated. Schoolmasters were to train their pupils in the doctrines contained in one of his father's favourite books, which had already been prescribed as a text-book in his father's reign, the book entitled *Deus et Rex*. There were not a few in England among Laud's own men who would have regarded the Canons as a good book for England, as a commendable revision of the existing law. But their whole trend was alien to the Scottish tradition. It is not surprising that there seems to have been no attempt to give effect to the new constitution, though it might have been enforced at the instance of the younger bishops, had not the uproar over the Liturgy followed so hard on its heels.

THE PREFACE

The most radical departure from the Canons of 1604 is seen in the prefaced royal letter. In the earlier book this contains a record of the process by which the Church of England in lawful assembly had drawn up the canons, and then goes on to record their confirmation by King James. Now no such record was possible in this case, for the only official action ever taken by the Church was the appointment of a committee. And these canons were not its work. It was necessary, therefore, to preface them with the official letter of royal authorization. This followed the form set for the Church of England, of which the King was the acknowledged supreme governor. The central words are these : ' We do not only, by our Prerogative Royal and Supreme Authority in Causes Ecclesiastical, ratify and confirm, by these our Letters Patents, the said Canons, Orders, and Constitutions, and all and everything in them contained ; but likewise, we command, by our Authority Royal, and by these our Letters Patents, the same to be diligently observed and executed by our loving subjects of that our Kingdom, both within the provinces of St. Andrews and Glasgow, in all points wherein they do concern every, or any, of them, according to this our will and pleasure, hereby expressed and declared.'

Laud's own chaplain acknowledged that this manner of imposition was ' contrary to the usages of the Church in all times and ages.' A modern Scottish Episcopal historian has said bluntly that the Scottish Church ' was no more consulted than an African tribe would be to-day by a body of foreign missionaries engaged in their conversion.' Clarendon, one of Charles's most loyal supporters, says : ' It was a fatal inadvertency, that neither before nor after these canons were sent to the King were they seen by the Assembly or any convocation of the clergy, which was so strictly obliged to the observation of them ; nor so much as communicated to the Lords of the Council of that kingdom.' It was fatal certainly, but was it an inadvertency ? The whole structure of the Preface and the opening chapter suggest that it was a deliberate attempt to

6

exercise, and to extend the sphere of, the Royal Supremacy. For King Charles it was claimed that he had inherited the power ' that the godly kings had among the Jews.' His father's teaching had found one too apt disciple.

' UNDER THE CURTAIN '

Reference ought to be made to one cryptic remark in a letter from Archbishop Laud to Bishop Maxwell : ' I am very glad your Canons are in so good a readiness, and that the true meaning of that one Canon still remains under the curtain. I hope you will take care that it may be fully printed and passed with the rest. It will be of great use for the settling of the Church.' Which canon were Laud and Maxwell keeping hid from even their warmest supporters ? It cannot have been the one above mentioned aimed at Bellenden of Aberdeen, for Bellenden had been warned of the King's displeasure. It cannot have been the one prescribing the Translation of King James as the sole version of the Bible to be used in worship. For all men knew that the Geneva version was completely out of favour. It seems to me [1] that it must have been Chapter VIII, where, after giving what seems full and final authority to National Synods, it expressly prohibits them from ' altering any Rubric, Article, Canon Doctrinal or Disciplinary whatsover.' In these matters their power was limited to conveying representations to His Majesty. Thus no bishop or group of bishops in the Church, not even the Church acting in its

---

[1] This, which in 1936 was a pure inference, without contemporary documentary evidence, was confirmed five years later in the writings of Laud himself (v, p. 49 *infra*).

corporate capacity, was to have power to alter any Rubric in the Prayer-book when it came from the royal hand. No wonder this was kept 'under the curtain'! While it may be freely admitted that in these Canons the King was seeking what he really deemed to be the good of the Scottish Church, nevertheless, not only in the method of authorization, but in the contents, open and unavowed, the book of 1636 was a gauntlet flung by royal absolutism in the face of a Church and a people reared in a tradition of independence. Acceptance of the challenge was inevitable, but it did not come till the second gauntlet was thrown.

THE NATIONAL COVENANT OF 1638

EVERY great event in history becomes in course of time the prey of the maker of legends. It comes to be pranked out with all manner of sentimental accretions held at the moment to be artistic decorations, but seen later to be useless disfigurements. The signing of the National Covenant has suffered much in this respect at the hands of its friends. It has been made to carry more fringes and tassels than a mid-Victorian mantelpiece. When last a centenary was celebrated in Scotland this process was at its height. About that time there emerged the popular legend of the first subscriber. ' An aged nobleman, the venerable Earl of Sutherland, at last stepped slowly and reverentially forward, and with throbbing heart and trembling hand subscribed Scotland's Covenant with God.' Further, a new vogue was then given to the older legend of the ' assembled multitude of both sexes ' of every class and condition and age, in Greyfriars Churchyard with its appropriate pendant of the Covenant laid out for signature on a ' level gravestone.' The picture as it had grown found its most popular expression in the lines of Mrs. Menteath :

Oh ! Arthur's Seat gave back the shout of that assembled
    crowd,
As one bare forth the mighty bond, and many wept aloud ;
They spread it on a tombstone head (a martyr slept
    beneath),
And some subscribed it with their blood, and added
    ' Until death.'

How hard it is to cut oneself free of legend, once it has crept in, is evidenced by the very latest account (that of Agnes Mure MacKenzie) in which the sentimental accretions accepted as history have almost blotted out the original significance. 'On the 28th of February 1638, the Covenant was produced at a great open-air meeting in the Greyfriars Kirkyard of Edinburgh, below the Castle. Henderson prayed and Loudon made a speech, and the long document was then read aloud and presented for public signature. There was a high pitch of enthusiasm, and it was signed by large numbers not only of men but of women and children, some of the latter being under ten years.'

Edinburgh saw no such scene on Wednesday, 28th February 1638. What did happen on that day has been fully described by men who took part in it, and reveals it as one of the decisive days in the history of the Scottish Church, of the Scottish people, and even, one might say, of the political development of Western civilization.

This commemorative article has no space for detailing the ways in which James I, on the throne of England, sought not only to assimilate the Scottish Church to the English, but to indoctrinate his Northern people with the Divine Right of Kings. How many to-day have read *God and the King*, which was prescribed as a catechism for Scottish children ? But James knew Scotland, and had a shrewd sense of the limits to which he could go in translating his theory into practice. His son Charles, with a greater goodwill towards the Scottish Church, had no such sense. His Act of Revocation and the compromise which followed it, his totally unconstitutional and unacceptable Book of Canons, and finally his Liturgy, everywhere regarded as Canterbury amended by Rome, and his obstinate persistence in them, despite all remonstrance, public and private, had alienated the hearts of his Northern subjects of all classes and of almost every district.

The final crisis which called forth the Covenant took place in Stirling on 19th February. There a Proclamation was read in which Charles assumed full personal responsibility for the obnoxious Canons and Liturgy. Despite the haste and secrecy of the proceedings, the organized opposition was ready with a solemn protest. Hitherto they had held to the position that the Scottish bishops had been responsible and that Charles, when better informed, would repudiate his advisers. Such an assumption was no longer possible. Some decisive action was needed to bring their King to a better mind. He must be made to see that the whole nation was united in resistance, and that any hopes he might have entertained of dividing the opponents of his innovations was futile.

There was a general rally to Edinburgh to decide what was to be done. When the scheme of a Covenant was mooted there seems to have been general approval. It was resolved to take as a basis the anti-papal Covenant of 1581, and to bring it up to date. On 23rd February the work began. It was assigned to Johnston of Warriston to draw up the second part, a rehearsal of all the Acts of Parliament by which the Presbyterian Church had been established, and contrary errors renounced ; and to Alexander Henderson of Leuchars to draw up the third part, the actual Covenant to be sworn to. Certain noblemen seem to have been appointed to revise their work. In three days it was ready for submission.

Tuesday, 27th February, was the real day of testing. Was this a document on which all could unite? Or would there be a dissentient minority? It was read first to the nobles, 'in John Galloway's house,' says Rothes. Some small objections were made, and some phrases adjusted. Then, in the afternoon, the ministers gathered in the Tailor's Hall. The amended document was submitted to the commissioners of Presbyteries 'in the summer-house in the yaird' and after discussion and slight amendment, approved. The amended draft was then read to the whole body of ministers, over 200 of them, and heartily endorsed. Here is the central part of Johnston of Warriston's account of that fateful day. 'I read Confession, Acts of Parliament, and Band to the nobles, by whom two words were changed. After noon with great fears we went to the ministry, and after two alterations and a discussion of all objections, we got it approved first by the commissioners (of Presbyteries) then by the whole ministry, except one.'

Approval having been thus secured, a scribe was set to work upon 'a fair parchment above an ellne in squair' to have a copy ready against the morrow. After further consultations in the forenoon of Wednesday, a meeting was called for Greyfriars Church at two in the afternoon. There, after devotional exercises by Alexander Henderson, and a speech by Loudon, Johnston of Warriston produced the Covenant. At four o'clock the signing began—the noblemen beginning and after them the 'barrons.' It was nearly eight when the last had signed. From the contemporary accounts it is perfectly plain that all the proceedings of that afternoon were within the church, and that the gathering consisted of the nobility, greater and lesser, of the realm. It is perfectly plain also that scribes were set to work that night to pen other copies, that the signing of the ministers began on the next day in the Tailor's Hall, and that of the other delegates and visitors to Edinburgh on Friday, the 2nd of March. From the available evidence it appears that it was not until the 1st of April that any general signing began in Edinburgh, though during March there were notable scenes elsewhere.

The sober fact, then, is that on that 28th of February three hundred years ago there was in Greyfriars Church a great gathering of resolute men—the representative lay leaders of the Scottish people, putting their names to a document every phrase of which had been carefully scrutinized and debated, with the full knowledge that they were taking a decisive step. They had been driven into a corner, and every word of the third part—the 'Band,' as Johnston calls it—shows how determined they were neither to be coerced nor divided. They recognize that 'the foul aspersions of rebellion and combination' will be put upon them. But they are determined to uphold the former purity of religion, and to resist the recent innovations to the uttermost of their powers all the days of their lives. They have neither intention nor desire, they continue, to diminish 'the King's greatnesse and authority.' On the contrary, they will stand to the defence of His Majesty 'in the defence and preservation of the foresaid true Religion, liberties and Lawes of the Kingdome.' Then follows the crucial clause. What if

King Charles persists in refusing to listen to his banded people, and continues to lend his ear to those whose advice has brought matters to this pass? How are they to phrase unmistakably yet politely, their determination to stand by their laws and liberties, whatever happens? The clause that finally emerged from the crucible was a pledge to stand ' also to the mutual defence and assistance every one of us of another, in the same cause of maintaining the true religion and His Majesty's Authority, with our best counsel, our bodies, meanes, and whole power, against all sorts of persons whatsoever.' Nothing was to divide them from ' this blessed and loyal conjunction.'

As we know, the thing they dreaded came to pass. Charles, if impressed at all, had gone too far to retract. His subtle schemes for dividing them and his two campaigns failed to penetrate their solid front. Within two years they had obtained all they had sworn to defend and more. For the bishops themselves were swept away, along with the innovations for which they were not responsible, but of which they allowed themselves to be the instruments. If Crawford is right, Archbishop Spottiswoode saw this from the very day of the first signatures. ' We have been making a tub these fourty years, and now the bottom thereof is fallen out.'

Division did come later, when the Civil War broke out in England, and the two factions there found counterparts in Scotland. But the second Band—the Solemn League and Covenant—with its mingled coercions and heroisms and martyrdoms is not relevant to this article.

The National Covenant was a document in which

stern determination and legal dexterity were blended.
The phrases culled from it to its discredit are all from
the older part which James promoted, and Charles
did not scruple to use. It achieved its aims immediately,
and also ultimately. And one cannot look on any of the
ancient fading copies, whether in Huntly House, the
National Library, New College, or elsewhere, without
feeling in close contact with one of the landmarks of
human history. It made a breach in the walls of
arbitrary royal despotism which led to its final over-
throw. But totalitarian claims like those of Charles
find to-day other embodiments than kings ; and the
modern application of Scotland's Covenant-experience
may be made in those words of Sir Charles Grant
Robertson in his Beckly Lecture for 1937 : 'The
totalitarian rulers are really right in their fear that a
true and free Christian Church within the State will
in the end be an acid dissolving the foundations of
totalitarian power and authority.'

ADDRESS IN GREYFRIARS: TERCENTENARY CELEBRATION, 27TH FEBRUARY 1938

IT is recorded of Ezra the Scribe that, when he was inaugurating a recall to religion, he brought forth the book of the law of Moses, read it aloud distinctly, and gave the sense, and caused the people to understand the reading. Perhaps the most fitting celebration of the great event which has gathered us together would be to bring forth the National Covenant as signed in this church three centuries ago, to read it aloud distinctly as was done on that historic day, and to give the sense with clearness. But it might not prove quite so simple as it sounds. So many words and phrases would need elucidation that our gathering might be even more prolonged than the one it commemorates.

We must, therefore, find another way of honouring the occasion, met as we are to acknowledge our debt, as churchmen and as citizens, to ancestors who, in the worst days of Stuart despotism, rose to the height of an unparalleled challenge—and who, after fifty years of conflict, secured for their descendants the rights and liberties, at times so conspicuously denied to themselves.

' Woe unto you, when all men shall speak well of you,' said our Lord. Neither in their own generation nor in any generation since have the Covenanters stood in any danger of this woe. With a multitude of admirers and hero-worshippers, they have never lacked opponents nor detractors. Nor is this to be wondered at. There were some strange creatures in the period. Every live movement possesses a fatal fascination for the discontented and the crank ; and, in addition, a generation of repression works havoc in any party and produces strange reactions in some of the less stable among its genuine adherents. But that one should judge the Covenanters by Muckle John Gib or Margaret Mitchelson, would be as ridiculous as to assess the prophetic movement in Israel by the plausible Hananiah, or the cocksure Zedekiah with his symbolic horns of iron.

A more serious charge is that the sermons and writings of even the best of the Covenanters are in places offensive in language, and even in thought, to the sensitive mind. Their massive expositions and weighty treatises have always been less well-known in certain circles than the spicy collections of passages, genuine and apocryphal, which were compiled in malice, and industriously circulated for the delectation of palates south of the Border. But, as Dr. McCrie showed long ago, they had no monopoly of such aberrations. Their wildest vagaries can be matched, and indeed overmatched, in the sermons and works of their opponents. However foreign they seem to us, they were an accepted part of the homiletics and the polemics of the time.

A still more serious charge is that, in the short heyday of their power in the 1640's, they acted with a tyranny and an oppression which was no less conspicuous than that against which they had risen. This is a charge which has more to say for itself. They certainly were led to embark on courses from which they would have shrunk in horror at the outset. And though they passionately protested that there was all the difference in the world between *two* kinds of uniformity—the one to which they had been subjected—imposed from without in contravention of their constitutional inheritance ; and the other which they were endeavouring to secure —in a régime of the true Reformation tradition in harmony with the laws and liberties of the realm ; though, further, it would be easy to multiply parallels to this change of attitude throughout the Christian centuries and hard to find one instance of ideals fully sustained in an hour of triumph, yet to use coercion in such a high cause as theirs was radically indefensible. To say that the best of us would have done the same may be true enough, but it does not exculpate them, it only condemns ourselves.

For generations there was controversy in Scotland as to whether intolerant and persecuting principles were not embedded in the very documents of the Covenant period. 'They were,' said some, 'and we repudiate these documents in so far as they set them forth.' 'They were not,' said others, 'and no fair interpretation can discern them.' Both positions were maintained with voluminous plausibility. But it would serve no purpose to rake up the embers of forgotten controversy. Its very existence in the ranks of men who honoured the Covenanters as one main fountainhead of their corporate life, indicates that they were children of their age, however much they contributed to its advance.

With all admissions and qualifications, grudging or spontaneous, the Covenant movement as a whole was one for which any nation might well display its banners, and it will be a sad day for Scotland when the very name ' Covenanter ' fails to call forth a generous patriotic pride.

But the special object of our commemoration to-day is not the half-century of struggle, but the deed which gave it birth. Within this church, on a Wednesday afternoon three centuries ago to-morrow, the National Covenant first saw the light and was signed by a thoroughly representative gathering of determined men. In the presence of God, Scotland's leading men set their names to a document which was to have lasting effects, both civil and religious. It may be contended that the political repercussions were more dramatic and more widespread over the English-speaking world ; it may be that it is impossible to disentangle the others from them ; but I feel drawn to make the attempt, and to concentrate to-day on its religious and ecclesi-astical bearings. But I would like to do so, bearing in mind these words of a modern political thinker, pondering the problems raised by the totalitarian state of to-day : ' The spiritual freedom which the Church demands and without which the Christian religion and the Christian Church cannot exist, can neither be secured nor exercised without securing and exercising other freedoms—intellectual, moral, political, social and economic—and, in demanding and fighting for that spiritual freedom, the Christian is fighting also for freedoms to be enjoyed by those who may remain indifferent, or are antagonistic, to the Christian re-ligion.' In concentrating, therefore, on the religious aspects, we are neither denying nor belittling the others. With this in view, I desire to focus attention on three points.

Firstly, the crisis that called forth the Covenant was primarily a religious issue. It was on the Church that the King's heaviest hand was laid. It was against *her* liberties that the main menace was directed. I am not ignoring that there were other grounds for restiveness—threats to the pockets of some landlords, changes in the constitution of the Privy Council and the Lords of the Articles, and the like—but these were purely secondary. In all the documents of the Covenant period there are three things continually held up to reprobation as the evils against which all Scotland must unite : the Canons which were to transform the very constitution of the Church, the Liturgy which was to change the nature of her worship, and the refurbished Court of High Commission, which was to be the instrument of compulsion.

It was fortunate for Scotland that the very first offender to be dealt with saw the issues so clearly. This was a middle-aged minister of a country parish who had taken no real lead before—Alexander Henderson of Leuchars. Threatened with outlawry for not being in possession of two copies of the Service-book for the use of his parish, he emerged from the seclusion of that parish to appeal to the Privy Council against the justice of the sentence. And the document he presented to that body went to the roots of the matter and succinctly stated the grounds of the widespread resistance which was becoming daily more apparent, and the policy on which that resistance was to concentrate. There are five reasons in all, and the central one—the third—is central in more senses than one. Here it is. ' Thirdly, the Kirk of Scotland is an independent Kirk, and her own pastors should be most able to decern and direct what do best seem our measure of reformation, and what may serve most for the good of the people.' The other four points illustrate how this fundamental principle of the autonomy of the Church has been infringed. No General Assembly has been summoned to consider the innovations ; no Parliament has approved of them ; they are manifestly contrary to the legal constitution of the Church as determined by the Church and confirmed by Parliament ; further, they all tend in a Romeward direction, and a people taught as the people of Scotland have been, will never accept them, even though the pastors acquiesce.

It was no mere question, Henderson saw clearly, of the comparative merits of two liturgies, or the rival claims of two forms of organization. If it were conceivable that new canons like those of 1636 had been introduced constitutionally or that a liturgy resembling that of 1637 had appeared with regular Scottish ecclesiastical sanction, it is also conceivable that Henderson would have acquiesced. But the whole manner of their introduction struck at the spiritual autonomy inherent in the very nature of the Church 'without which the Christian Church would cease to be either Christian or a Church.' So, even although the Canons pronounced excommunication on those who refused to the King's Majesty the same authority in causes ecclesiastical 'that the godlie kings had amongst the Jews ' ; undeterred by this threat, and unmoved by this distinct hint of lack of respect for the Word of God, the Scottish Church, led by Henderson, refused to give up its birthright and to be disloyal to its Head. We rightly honour their heroic stand, just as we honour those who in the Confessional Church in Germany to-day—aye, and in the Roman Catholic Church there—are resisting similar pressures amid even more urgent perils.

But, secondly, the mainspring of the resistance was religious. When the lay leaders of the people signed the Covenant here in Greyfriars, it was open to the unsympathetic observer to say that it was just another ebullition on the part of these turbulent barons of Scotland who had been creating trouble all down its history. But no such interpretation can explain the enthusiasm with which the Covenant was welcomed in almost every corner of the land. The fervour and unanimity of those subsidiary days of swearing and of signing astonished even the most optimistic. Scotland was swept by a movement unparalleled in its force. It was no cowed ignorant peasantry moving at the crack of the whip of its feudal overlords. It was a genuine uprising of latent religious sentiment.

The leaders of the movement were bent on showing the King that they did not stand alone. But none of them, in their rosiest dreams, expected the response that followed. It means that there must have been generations of effective religious teaching. We are so apt to think that men like Robert Bruce and David Dickson and Samuel Rutherford were almost unsupported in their work. Yet there must have been a host of faithful men in quiet parishes who were solidly educating their people in the Reformation-Gospel and the implications of that Gospel. For, in the main, the response was not mechanical or unthinking, but intelligent and considered. Bishop Gilbert Burnet, speaking of his early days in the heart of the Covenant movement, said, ' We were indeed amazed to see a poor commonalty so capable to argue upon points of Government and on the bounds to be set to the power of princes in matters of religion; upon all these topics they had texts of Scripture at hand, and were ready with the answers to anything that was said to them. This measure of knowledge was spread even among the meanest of them, their cottagers and their servants.'

I wonder to what extent any religious issue would receive the same intelligent backing in Scotland to-day. Would it disclose the same background of solid teaching in quiet places ? Would it, despite all our advantages, reveal such a firm grasp of essential principles ? I only ask the question. It might be that we would be just as surprised at the answer as the men of that generation were.

At no time in Scottish history, however, not even in the seventeenth century, can we flatter ourselves that Scotland would have presented a united front on any issue on religious grounds alone. So it cannot be denied that other motives entered in. There were those who were moved by an early brand of Scottish Nationalism. They felt that although a Stuart king ruled in London, it was *from London* that he ruled, and Scotland was fast becoming a mere appendage to England. Though true-born Englishmen were all the time complaining of needy Scots adventurers taken up into the royal favour, their fellow-countrymen reckoned them denationalized, having lost their sense of country, though they had not lost their accent.

But further, in every generation of our history there have been men to whom neither religion nor patriotism meant anything. Nothing would move them but self-interest, some hope of enrichment, or some fear of deprivation. A few men of this type signed the Covenant. Though the threat of the Act of Revocation had passed, some felt that it might prove the harbinger of other raids on property, on the part of an absentee king. So Charles was confronted with a practically unanimous opposition because, in addition to his attack on the liberties of the Kirk, he had outraged national sensibilities, and made sundry upstart lairds alarmed at the prospect of confiscations.

The mainspring, however, of the national resistance was religion ; apart from it the movement would never have begun, nor would it have kept going and gathering momentum.

But not only was the crisis that called forth the Covenant primarily a religious issue, not only was the mainspring of the movement religious, but the Covenant itself is a religious document. Now, someone casually turning over the pages of the Covenant for the first time (for I need hardly remind you that, although the original Covenant was penned carefully on *one* fair sheet of parchment of goodly size, it occupies several pages in a modern book), one turning over its pages, I say, and dipping into it, might wonder at this description. His eye might be caught by the first part—the original Covenant of 1581—and running over its amazing list of things repudiated, he might wonder what this had to do with religion. But just as every positive enactment of the present day has to be accompanied by a clause stating that all previous legislation bearing on this subject is thereby repealed in so far as it is contrary to the new enactment, so the noble positive statement of faith in the Scots Confession of 1560 had as its pendant this negative Confession of 1581, detailing explicitly the doctrines and practices which had been renounced.

Or his eye might linger on the second part, and he might wonder what all this lengthy catalogue of Acts of Parliament had to do with religion. But if he took the trouble to look them up in the statute-book he would find that, for the most part, they were the varied legal confirmations of the Church's position and decisions ; and further, that they demonstrated the constitution and worship of the Church as legally acknowledged to be of such a nature that the late innovations were foreign to her genius.

But as to the third part—the effective part—the Covenant proper, he would not have an instant's hesitation. It is manifestly a great religious pronouncement. That was only to be expected in a work of Alexander Henderson's. It is permeated by the quiet, profound fervour of his piety which radiates through its cumbrous sentences. It is a most solemn engagement before God to seek one end, ' to recover the purity and liberty of the Gospel, as it was established and professed ' before the late innovations. And in pursuit of that end—let me recall its significant phrases— ' We promise and swear by the Great Name of the Lord our God ' ' that we shall defend the foresaid religion ' ' to the uttermost of the power that God hath put in our hands, all the days of our life.' ' And in like manner ' ' we promise and swear that we shall ' ' stand to the defence of our dread sovereign the King's Majesty, his person and his authority, *in the defence of* the foresaid true religion, liberties, and laws of the kingdom,' ' as also to the mutual defence and assistance every one of us of another ' ' *against all sorts of persons whatsoever.*'

This meant a deliberate preparation for all eventualities—a costly step to take—and one not taken lightly, but with much searching of heart in the sight of God. It is Scotland's echo of Martin Luther's ' Here I stand. I can no other. So help me God.'

And then, at the close, after every detailed pledge has been piled up to secure unity and steadfastness in the common cause, there is the moving final paragraph. It is rarely quoted or referred to in histories of the Covenant, for it seems to have no direct bearing on the political and ecclesiastical aims of the signatories. But in the eyes of Henderson it had, and *this one sentence* from it I cannot refrain from quoting. ' And because we cannot look for a blessing from God upon our proceedings, except with our profession and subscription we join such a life and conversation as becometh Christians who have renewed their Covenant with God : We therefore faithfully promise for ourselves, our followers, and all others under us, both in public and in our particular families and personal carriage, to endeavour to keep *ourselves* within the bounds of Christian liberty, and to be good examples to others, of all godliness, soberness, and righteousness, and of every duty we owe to God and man.'

To Henderson, effective witness in a religious cause demanded religious men. He may have been disappointed in many who took this pledge, but others there were on whom it left its mark for ever. 1638 and the years that followed saw, among other things, a striking revival of religion. The recall of the Covenant had not been sounded in vain.

Long after the National Covenant had achieved its end, and when its later satellite, the Solemn League and Covenant, was a relic of a vanished past, it was the custom, in certain circles in Scotland, to meet for a renewal of the Covenants. In some of these circles this meant that they asserted the perpetual obligation of these Covenants as they stood ; but in most it meant that they recalled them with pride and gratitude, and adapted the old-time obligations to the issues of their own day. *Such* a renewal of the Covenants, when pursued with judgment and insight, *was a most salutary discipline*. It helped to keep religion alive in days when it seemed ready to perish. And while no one would seriously propose the restoration of that discipline as it was, who could predict the effect on the religion of our land if we, in this Church assembled, were this day to renew our vows unto the Lord our God in His presence and in the presence of all His people ; to honour our Covenanting forefathers not in word only, but in deed ; and with cleansed heart and rekindled zeal, to labour, with rededicated lives, to make this land of ours a land under homage to Christ ?

WILLIAM LAUD AND SCOTLAND

As a boy in an Ayrshire farmhouse—with ready access to the literature gathered by three generations of farmers of Covenanting and Secession stock—with an absolutely voracious appetite for everything written in prose and verse concerning our Scottish past—an appetite not deterred, even at a very tender age by the long s's and other conventions of the printing of an earlier day—I naturally accumulated alongside a private group of Scottish heroes, an equally imposing array of villains—not all Scottish but all impinging on our Scottish story. Two of these outdid all others —the 'fause' Menteith and William Laud. So far as I can recall, Blind Harry was responsible for the one, and the first sections of many Covenanting books for the other. All later apologies for the betrayer of Wallace have left me unimpressed, but my engrained contempt for Laud was stoutly shaken when a student. The agent who administered the shock was Wordsworth. That a mind so lofty, and so fearless in its judgment, should conceive a sonnet to the memory of Laud was a fact that had to be reckoned with. Many of you will recall that sonnet, but it may not have stunned you that the hand that penned ' Milton ! thou shouldst be living at this hour,' should also trace these words :

> Prejudged by foes determined not to spare
> An old weak man for vengeance thrown aside,

Laud, ' in the painful act of dying ' tried,
(Like a poor bird entangled in a snare
Whose heart still flutters, though his wings forbear
To stir in useless struggle) hath relied
On hope that conscious innocence supplied,
And in his prison breathes celestial air.
Why tarries, then, thy chariot ?   Wherefore stay,
O Death ! the ensanguined yet triumphant wheels,
Which thou prepar'st, full often, to convey,
(What time a State with madding faction reels)
The saint or patriot to the world that heals
All wounds, all perturbations doth allay ?

' *Conscious innocence,*' ' *celestial air,*' ' *saint or patriot.*'
These seemed strange words indeed to use of the Laud
that I had learned.

Some of you will remember that Wordsworth himself felt that his sonnet needed some justification. So
he prepared a note to be appended to it in every full
edition of his works. This note was no less disquieting :
' In this age a word cannot be said in praise of Laud,
or even in compassion for his fate, without incurring
a charge of bigotry ; but, fearless of such imputation,
I concur with Hume " that it is sufficient for his
vindication to observe that *his* errors were the most
excusable of all those that prevailed during that
zealous period." A key to the right understanding of
those parts of his conduct that brought the most odium
upon him in his own time, may be found in the following passage of his speech before the bar of the House
of Peers : " Ever since I came in place, I have laboured
nothing more than that the external worship of God,
so much slighted in divers parts of this kingdom, might
be preserved, and that with as much decency and

uniformity as might be. For I evidently saw that the public neglect of God's service in the outward face of it, and the nasty lying of many places dedicated to that service, *had almost cast a damp upon the true and inward worship of God, which, while we live in the body, needs external helps, and all little enough to keep it in vigour.*" '

From the time I encountered this sonnet my attitude to Laud began insensibly to alter ; I began to make excuses for him ; I came to believe that, in regard to Scotland at least, he was the victim of mistaken pre-suppositions ; that he had, to a great extent, the religious welfare of our country at heart ; and that, while his policy was disastrous, it could be attributed to two factors over which he had no control—viz. the ecclesiastical aims which King Charles had inherited from his father, and the radically unsound advice tendered to him by two Scottish prelates, Bishop Maxwell of Ross and Bishop Wedderburn of Dunblane. So, while not minimizing the catastrophe of 1637 in the slightest, I had come to shift the responsibility.

It was with these presuppositions that, a short time ago, I began a desultory but intensive study of the documents of the period ; and it was a genuine surprise to find that my more favourable estimate crumbled in the process, and that my earlier view had more ample justification than I had come to believe.

. . . . . .

Before we can appreciate with discrimination Arch-bishop Laud's relation to Scotland, it is necessary to remind ourselves what precisely his admirers claim that he achieved for the Church of England. May I lay before you what seem the two most representative favourable verdicts. One is practically contemporary

—the summing up, by his former chaplain Dr. Heylyn, in his *Cyprianus Anglicus*. ' If we look into the Church as it stood under his direction, we shall find the Prelates generally more intent upon the work committed to them, more earnest to reduce this Church to the ancient Orders, than in former times ; the Clergy more obedient to the commands of their *Ordinaries*, joining together to advance the work of *Uniformity* recommended to them ; the Liturgy more punctually executed in all the parts and offices of it ; the Word more diligently preacht, the Sacraments more reverently administred, than in some scores of years before ; the people more conformable to those Reverend Gestures in the House of God which, though prescribed before, were but little practised ; more cost laid out upon the beautifying and adorning of Parochial Churches, in furnishing and repairing Parsonage-houses, than at, or in all the times since, the Reformation ; the Clergy grown to such esteem, for parts and power, that the Gentry thought none of their Daughters to be better disposed of than such as they had lodged in the Arms of a Church-man ; and the Nobility grown so well affected to the State of the Church, that some of them designed their younger sons to the Order of Priesthood, to make them capable of rising in the same *Ascendant*.'

From this somewhat naïve seventeenth-century eulogy, we turn to that pronounced [by Rev. C. H. Simpkinson] at the Archbishop Laud Commemoration in 1895. ' This (viz. a sense of mission) is what marks off William Laud above all the famous ecclesiastics of that grand age, the saintly Andrewes, the politic Williams, the industrious Harsnet, the devout Cosin, the eloquent Calamy, the affectionate Baxter, as the one greatest man among them all, who had something to do and who did it, and who sealed it gladly with his blood, leaving a work behind him (which has lasted already two hundred and fifty years)—our beloved Church of England, Apostolic and liberal, devout and full of missionary zeal, national in organization, and œcumenical in sympathy ; so cautious to preserve all the ornaments which the long struggles of history have won, yet boldly stripping off the chains of that strange Roman slavery which, for a time, seemed even to great and good minds the necessary condition for success.'

It will be observed that three things stand out from these eulogies, the improved discipline of the Church, the rise in status of Churchmen, and the enrichment of worship, retaining much of the mediæval reverential splendour, while emphatically repudiating Rome. All three can be plausibly attributed to Laud, though each of them deserves a closer scrutiny.

He was indubitably a disciplinarian—the most unbending, indeed, in the history of the modern Church. He gloried in the efficiency of ' these two able governors *præmium* and *pœna* '—*præmium* in the shape of the speedy promotion of willing agents, *pœna* in the form of fines and imprisonments, and the indefensible practice of bodily mutilations. At his trial, he objected to the actions of the Star Chamber and the Court of High Commission being charged against him, but in all the most notorious of their sentences he was the moving spirit. He revived, amid much opposition, particularly from the See of Lincoln, the right of the Metropolitan to make visitations of the dioceses in his province, adducing mediæval precedent as his warrant. Before his day, many local variations had grown up in the celebration of public worship; Laud would have none. A disciplinarian certainly, but was he a sound one? Was the Uniformity he sought according to the recognized Canons of the Church? It would be hard to justify this claim, as will appear a little later. Burton, who was set in the pillory and had his ears cropped, uttered, in the sermon for which he was condemned, one very penetrating remark, that Laud 'had a Papal infallibility of spirit, whereby, as by a Divine Oracle, all Questions in Religion are finally determined.' It was not the element of discipline, but the fact that men felt that they were being dragooned according to the wayward standards of a dominant spirit backed by the Royal prerogative, that led to his imprisonment and death.

Next, did he raise the status of Churchmen? In one sense, yes. Churchmen held a place in the Councils of Charles I that they had never attained since the Reformation. They filled many of the highest offices of State, and not without credit. There is one illuminating entry in Laud's diary for 1636. 'Sunday, March 6: William Juxon, Lord Bishop of London, made Lord High Treasurer of England. No Churchman had it since Henry VII's time; I pray God bless him to carry it so that the Church may have honour, and the King and the State service and contentment by it. And now if the Church will not hold up themselves, under God I can doe no more.' The same tendency is apparent in Scotland under the Laudian régime. There is no doubt that in this Laud was convinced that he was doing the Church a real service. As Professor Mozley has pointed out in his essay on Laud, he was haunted 'by a sacerdotal political form

33

of a Church in power, her orders nobility, her prelates pillars of the State.' But how, in point of fact, did it fare with their ecclesiastical duties ? It is a remarkable thing that, though at the moment 'bishopping' was being pressed in Scotland, I can find no trace in Laud's Diary of his having ever conducted a Confirmation service.[1] And while some of these civil appointments carried with them quite adequate emoluments, those Churchmen who looked forward to them had to haunt the Court in advance. This meant two things —considerable expenditure, and partial neglect of their cures. Pluralism was rampant. A disciplinarian like Laud might have been expected to deal with this evil. And one is led to expect it from his Diary where under June 19, 1621, we read : 'His Majesty gave me the grant of the bishopric of St. David's.' ' The King gave me leave to retain the presidentship of St. John's College in my *commendam* with the bishopric. But by reason of the strictness of that statute, which I will not violate, nor my oath to it, under any colour, I am resolved before my consecration to leave it.' Here, it seems, is no pluralist. But the Diary also reveals that he administered his Welsh diocese from London, making only two brief visits in five years ; and that concurrently with it he was Dean of Gloucester, a prebend of Westminster, a prebend of Lincoln, and held in addition three country livings. The bulk of modern Anglo-Catholics have a sensitive conscience in regard to the cure of souls ; when they exalt Laud they must turn a blind eye to this aspect of his career. If we are to

---

[1] Indeed, one of the charges against the Bishops in the Long Parliament was ' that they had laid aside the use of *confirming* Children, though required by law.'

credit Laud with improving the status of Churchmen, we must pay regard exclusively to civil reputation, and not to spiritual efficiency.

The third claim made for Laud takes us into most debatable territory—that he achieved the enrichment of worship, retaining much of the mediæval reverential splendour, while emphatically repudiating Rome. This would furnish material for a monograph, rather than the few paragraphs which can here be allotted. There was no point on which Laud was more insistent at his trial than the stupidity and malice of the charge of a desire on his part to return to the Roman obedience and to take his country with him. True, he had more than once received the offer of a Cardinal's hat, but that he had quite definitely refused on the ground 'that something dwelt within him, which would not suffer that, till Rome were other than it is.' True, also, he had discouraged the identification of the Pope with Antichrist and eschewed all provocative epithets. But what Divine of the Church of England, he asked, had ever been responsible for more conversions from Rome? Was not his conference with Fisher the Jesuit a decisive answer to the exclusive claim of the Roman See? The fact that he had repudiated Geneva was no indication of an inclination towards Rome. What right had his accusers to regard Calvin as the only genuine non-Roman? 'The Catholic Church of Christ is neither Rome nor a conventicle.' Certainly Laud repudiated Rome, but this did not alter the conviction of his opponents, both English and Scottish, that his inclination was Romewards. Formally, it appeared in his constant appeal to pre-Reformation practice ; materially, in the character of the innovations most closely connected with his name. These centre round the Holy Table, its place in the Church, and the reverence to be paid to it. As finally crystallized into the canons of 1640, these seem comparatively harmless. There the position of the Communion Table is declared to be ' in its own nature indifferent ' ; that ' no religion is to be placed therein, or scruple to be made thereon.' Further, this position under the East window of the Chancel ' doth not imply that it is or ought to be esteemed a true and proper altar, whereon Christ is again really sacrificed ; but it is and may be called an altar by us, in that sense which the Primitive Church called it an altar, and no other.' Further, it is to ' be decently severed with rails ' to save it from profanation. Yet, rails or not, liberty is preserved for the bishop to move it during the time of celebration. Finally, the ancient custom of obeisance towards the altar is ' heartily commended to the serious considera-tion of all good and well-affected people.' This is the gist of what Laud induced his somewhat irregular Convocation to pass in 1640. But this was after more than twenty years of constant striving to restore the altar, during which time his whole attitude was very different. He began in Gloucester Cathedral in 1616, the year he was appointed Dean. He ordered the Communion Table to be placed altarwise against the wall, and he required of all the church officials, seeing they now had an altar, to make ' their humble rever-ence to Almighty God ' as they approached it, ' accord-ing to the laudable custom of the Primitive times.' Thenceforward he was consistent. Wherever he had, or could claim, authority, his way had to be followed. Now, since the Prayer-book contained no hint of this, where did Laud find plausible grounds for his action ? At Gloucester he seems to have adduced three : the custom of the Chapel Royal, the lay-out of some other cathedrals, and the will of King James. When the controversy became fierce, he fell back on the Elizabethan Injunctions of 1559. Into the question of the validity of these Injunctions in the time of Charles I there is no need to enter. Laud relied on the one for ' Tables in the Church,' and stressed this clause ' that the holy table in every church be decently made, and set in the place where the altar stood,' and lightly passed over the other provisions that it was ' so to stand, saving when the Communion of the Sacrament is to be administered,' and that ' after the communion done, from time to time the same holy table to be placed where it stood before.' The more Puritan clergy naturally asked why, if Laud regarded the Injunctions as still operative, he did not enforce the whole Injunction, and why he ignored others, like the 23rd concerning the destruction of ' shrines . . . and all other monuments of idolatry and superstition . . . in walls, glass windows, or elsewhere.' The debate within the Church was bitter, and some of its incidents are best forgotten. There was no hope of an agreed canon to Laud's mind. So, to drive his way, he fell back on the King as Supreme Governor of the Church, and induced Charles to enter the field on his behalf. When the Canon of 1640 said that the position of the table was ' in its nature indifferent,' and that genuflection to it was only to be ' heartily commended to serious consideration ' ' as an ancient and laudable custom ' it was definitely resiling from Laud's constant contention. To him it was no matter of indifference, nor was

genuflection before the altar to be pretermitted by any
loyal Churchman. He had consistently directed that
bodily reverence should be made towards the altar in
its restored position. In his famous speech to the
Star Chamber he used an *Argumentum ad homines*.
Addressing the Knights of the Garter present, he
reminded them, that when, in their great solemnities
they did reverence to Almighty God, traditionally, it
was ' towards His altar, as the greatest place of God's
residence on earth,' and that, by their oath (a pre-
Reformation oath which had remained unchanged)
they were bound to give due honour and reverence
to God ' and to His altar.' And at his trial he added,
' As for the Knights of the Garter, if they might do it
without superstition, I hope I and other men might
do so too. Especially since they were ordered by
Henry V to do it with great reverence, *ad modum
sacerdotum.*'

But beyond this solitary and dubious precedent, he
had one argument that he seems to have considered
unanswerable. He fell back on it at his trial. He had
said, and he stood to it, that ' the altar is the greatest
place of God's residence on earth, greater than the
pulpit ; for there 'tis *Hoc est Corpus Meum*, This is My
Body ; but in the other it is at most but *Hoc est Verbum
Meum*, This is My Word ; and a greater reverence is
due to the Body, than the Word, of the Lord.' Laud's
notorious distrust of preaching may be responsible for
this remarkable assertion ; and this particular argument for the primacy of the altar could only have
cogency in the case of one who had at least drawn near
to some form of the Roman doctrine of Transubstantiation.

I have concentrated on this one issue, for, though only one of many, it held a dominant place in Laud's ecclesiastical activities. He repudiated Rome, certainly, but it was his concurrent repudiation of Geneva which stirred him into action. As A. C. Benson has put it, ' He hated Protestantism the worse of the two, for he loved neither the soul of it nor the clothes it wore ; whereas, he was well satisfied with the trappings of Romanism.' It was his insistence on these ' trappings of Romanism ' that roused resistance in England ; he was enforcing them with a challenged warrant ; it was impossible in England to secure such a revision of Canons and Liturgy as would make his warrant unchallengeable. So he had to make shift by calling in the Church's Supreme Governor to his aid, but Charles, pliant as he was, and ready in any crisis to use his executive authority, was reluctant to widen the rift between himself and his subjects by straining that authority to cover legislation, as Laud would have wished him to do. Witness his bitter epitaph on Strafford, ' He served a mild and gracious Prince, who knew not how to be, nor to be made great.' If Laud's will had been so prevailing with the King, as outsiders believe it was, he would have made him great, by the full exercise of his power as ' God's immediate lieutenant on earth ' ; Laud's ideal would have been realized ; the worship of the Church of England would have been enriched by a return to many mediæval practices, and a uniformity in ' the ancient and laudable customs ' secured. The moment Laud was in prison the revolt against this reform, on which his heart had been set, broke forth. ' Reformation goes on . . . as hot as a toast,' wrote an observer in London.

'The Parliament men would not receive the Communion at St. Margaret's, Westminster . . . before the rails were pulled down, and the communion table was removed into the middle of the chancel.'

So whether or not we sympathize with the general trend of Laud's new (or rather revived) regulations for worship, the fact remains that he lacked both the general consent of the clergy and people, and the unmistakable legislative authorization which could override all opposition.

A careful study of the documents suggests that it is here—in this English situation—that we find the key to the puzzles connected with his Scottish policy.

Concerning the documents that are available for this study, there is one thing that must be said at the outset. When Laud came to his final trial before the House of Lords, all the charges that he had to meet related to his English administration. Every time his accusers adduced a Scottish instance, Laud pled the Act of Oblivion. On the ninth day, for instance, to a charge connected with an order for burning the Pacification with the Scots, he made answer, 'Howsoever, this concerns the Scottish business, and therefore to the Act of Oblivion I refer myself.' [1]

But at the time when he was committed to prison, Laud fully expected that he would definitely be called upon to answer the charges which had been brought against him by the Scots, in the form in which these had been transmitted to the English Parliament. In consequence, he devoted a great deal of time and

---

[1] The Act referred to is the Act of Pacification and Oblivion included in the Treaty of London, by which, save in the case of certain named 'incendiaries,' all previous hostility was to be 'reputed as if it had not been.'

thought to an effective answer. And the ' Troubles '
part of his *Troubles and Tryal* is largely occupied with
his very plausible explanation of all that had led to
the regrettable uproar in the North. Historians on
both sides of the Border have relied far too exclusively
on this apparently sincere narrative for their reading
of events. Even standard histories quote it as con-
clusive. But it was written years after with a view
to clearing himself ; and, unfortunately for Laud, contemporary documents to some extent survived, which
showed that he was drawing a fancy picture, not only
of the course of events, but also of his whole attitude
towards the Scots. He was particularly unfortunate
in that many of his ' side-papers ' in cipher, meant for
the eye of Wentworth alone, and ordered to be con-
signed to the flames, have appeared in the various
collections of Strafford papers.

A similar misfortune befell him at his trial, when he
was prepared to dissociate himself from some of the
least popular of the actions and utterances of his king.
The original drafts of the King's speeches were found
in his study at Lambeth. ' It was most unfortunate,'
he says, ' that they should be now found, and I had
not left them a being, but that I verily thought I had
destroyed them long since. But they were unhappily
found among the heaps of my papers.' ' I might
shuffle here and deny the making of them, for no
proof is offered, but that they are in my hand ; and
that is no necessary proof.'

It would be a useful and rewarding task for some
young historian to examine Laud's answer to the
Scottish charges in the light of ascertained fact. Had
it been published at the time it would not have

escaped a searching scrutiny. But by 1694, when the *Troubles and Tryal* first saw the light, the Scottish interest in Laud had greatly waned, and no one seems to have thought it worth an answer. No one dreamt how much it was destined to colour the English and even the Scottish reading of the beginnings of the Covenanting struggle in days to come.

It is fitting, at this point, to illustrate this discrepancy. In his adroit defence, Laud does not conceal his conviction that the Scots were a wrong-headed and ungrateful people, but he does plausibly insinuate that the worst provocations they received were not from him, and that he was at all times a moderating influence restraining violent action against them. He shifts on to the King's shoulders responsibility for the enjoined wearing of whites, the removal of church galleries to make way for altars, the final form of the Liturgy, and the Public Prayers against the Scots. And here are some of his other statements. 'But as for the affairs of that Kingdom (though I had the honour to be a sworn Counsellor of that State as well as this), yet I never meddled with them, but at such time, and in such a way, as I was called and commanded by His Majesty.' 'I kindled no war against them, but kept it off from them as much and as long as I could.' 'I had no malignity answerable to their bitterness against the Church of England, nor did the "entering upon a new war" proceed from my counsels.' 'I have spoken nothing of them, but in prayer, that God will be pleased to turn all these things to the good and peace of both kingdoms ; which must be little less than a miracle, if He do.' Looking back from his prison, Laud saw himself an injured innocent, blamed for the misdeeds of others, but himself full of love and goodwill towards his alienated and misguided brethren.

But what is the evidence of his contemporary correspondence? In his 'side-papers' to Wentworth, with the cipher 197 for Scotland, we find a very different picture. 'I think as you do, 197 (Scotland) is the veriest devil that is out of hell.' 'All the Scotch horrid business . . . will remain to posterity the foulest blot that was ever dashed upon the Protestant churches. . . . Oh, my Lord, that you knew how the King hath been used in this business; though the truth is it hath been let alone too long.' 'All this hath happened by not treading out sparks before the flame broke out. Now I see no honourable way but force. . . . The King hath been shamefully betrayed in this business, and will I doubt ever be, in these half ways.' 'The want of "thorough" in a time of opportunity is cause of all.' 'For their lion is *rampant* . . . but the truth is, our lions are too *passant*.' '102 (I) did constantly call upon this business . . . and yet could not prevail with 100 (the King). 'Vigour and order may reduce this fellow 197 (Scotland) easily. But, surely, if this summer settle not the mind of the man, it will be ill dealing with him after he have broken his chain in Bedlam.' This clandestine correspondence—totally unknown to them—justifies the Scots Commissioners' impression that the blameless lamb was the main fomenter of strife. If he had had his way, Charles would have struck more quickly and more decisively. 'Thorough' would have been his motto. Enough has been said to indicate that too much weight can easily be put on Laud's later recapitulation of his dealings with Scotland and of the attitude he had adopted to the Scottish crisis.

There is one other matter that is clear from his correspondence. He had a definite animus against Scotsmen. His pen-portraits of all the leading representatives of our nation are etched with virulence. At some point early in his career he had acquired a complex against the whole tribe of them. Was it due to the fairy-tales with which King James regaled English audiences about the doings of Scottish Churchmen? Or, as a true-born Englishman, did he resent the presence of so many Anglified Scotsmen in the royal retinue? Or is there something more definite, of the nature of his encounters with Archie Armstrong, licensed jester first to King James and then to his royal son? The two main ones are worth recalling. On one of Laud's first visits to the Court, Archie Armstrong was ordered to say grace at the royal table. This he did in these words, ' All praise to God, and little Laud to the deil.' The other is later, and has sounder contemporary evidence. On his way into the first Privy Council meeting after word had come of the National Covenant, Archie Armstrong met Laud and said, ' News from Scotland, your Grace; who is the fool now? ' Laud felt that this was overstepping even the jester's privilege. So he was at once brought before the Council, and it was solemnly ordered ' by His Majesty, with the advice of the Board, that the jester should have his coat pulled over his head, and be discharged from the King's service, and banished the Court,' as is recorded in the Privy Council Register for 11th March 1638.

However early and unpleasant his encounters with Scotsmen may have been, Laud did not make his first contact with Scotland itself till 1617, when, as a junior ecclesiastical adviser, he accompanied King James in his only visit to his earliest subjects. This brief visit, from which he returned some time before the main party, receives practically no mention at all in his Diary, or any extant writing. But his later chaplain, Dr. Heylyn, has thus noted its main feature. The King had barely reached Edinburgh ' when the Presbyters conceiving that his coming was upon design to work an Uniformity between the Churches of both Kingdoms, set up one Struthers to preach against it, who laid so lustily about him in the chief Church of Edinburgh, that he not only condemned the *rites* and *ceremonies* of the Church of *England*, but prayed God to save *Scotland* from the same. Laud, and the rest of the chaplains who had heard the sermon, acquainted His Majesty with those passages ; but there was no remedy.' Now it does seem strange that the Scottish Church should have commissioned or permitted a tactless extremist to welcome the royal party in this brusque fashion. From Presbyterian sources it is just the opposite grumble that is heard. Wm. Struthers of St. Giles was regarded as a renegade, one who, from being a bitter enemy of the bishops, had degenerated into a royal pensioner and an aper of English ways. Calderwood never mentions him without some word of contempt. And here is his account of the King's first Sundays in Edinburgh. On the first Sunday ' in the Great Kirk, the Bishop of Saint Andrewes had a flattering sermon on the 21st Psalm.' And on the second Sunday in Edinburgh, ' Mr. William Struthers, one of the ministers of Edinburgh, preached this day in the chapell before the King, and observed the English form in his prayer and behaviour.' Heylyn almost makes one share Laud's disgust with the bad manners of the Scottish pulpit. But, reading Struthers's record, one is forced to ask, ' What did Laud expect of the Scottish Church, when one of its leading and most anglified ministers, doing his best to please his distinguished audience, is regarded as laying lustily about him against the whole Anglican position ? ' Heylyn also tells us that the King failed in the main object of his visit—to introduce the 5 Articles (which the following year became known as the 5 Articles of Perth) into the Scottish Church despite his blunt assertion at St. Andrews ' that it was a Power belonging to all Christian Princes to order matters in the Church ' ; but, he adds triumphantly, the failure was not for long, for ' His Majesty therefor took a better course, than to put the point to Argument and Disputation ; which was to beat them by the Belly, and to withdraw those Augmentations which he had formerly allowed them out of his Exchequer ; which Pill so wrought upon this indigent and obstinate People, that the next year . . . they passed the 5 Articles for which His Majesty had been courting them for two years together.' This comment illustrates the fact that Heylyn was a not inapt pupil of the devoted believer in *præmium* and *pœna* as instruments in promoting ecclesiastical obedience. There can be little doubt that Laud was not impressed with the comparatively cautious ways of King James in proceeding to his goal of conforming the Church of Scotland as closely as possible to that of England, for there is no real reason

to doubt the story which Bishop Hacket told in his
original unabridged biography of Archbishop Williams.
Williams at that time a bishop, and for ends of his
own, was pleading with the King that it was high time
that Laud was raised to a bishopric. He was met
with a definite refusal, for which, after some parleying,
the royal reasons were given : ' The plain truth is I
keep Laud back from all place of rule and authority
because I find he hath a restless spirit and cannot
see when matters are well, but loves to toss and change,
and to bring things to a pitch of reformation floating
in his own brain, which may endanger the steadfastness of that which, God be praised, is at a good pass.
I speak not at random : he hath made himself known
to me to be such an one. For when, three years past,
I had obtained of the Assembly of Perth to consent to
five articles of order and decency in a correspondence
with this Church of England, I gave them promise
that I would try their obedience no further anent
ecclesiastical affairs. Yet this man hath pressed me
to invite them to a nearer conjunction with the Liturgy
and Canons of this nation ; but I sent him back with
the frivolous draft that he had drawn.' This would
indicate that Laud was busying himself in drawing up
Canons and Liturgy for Scotland before 1621—that is
to say, eight years previous to that call from Bishop
Maxwell of Ross which he would have us believe was
the beginning of his concern for that country.

It is pertinent here to recall that the Scottish Church
had already been taking steps to review its constitution
and its worship. Indeed, the revision of Knox's Liturgy,
commissioned by the General Assembly of 1616, had
already been completed ; its nature and its history

can readily be gathered from G. W. Sprott's admirable edition. The same Assembly had resolved that there be ' ane uniforme ordour of Church discipline, and to that effect . . . a Book of Canons be made . . . drawin foorth of the bookis of former Assemblies.' What progress was made with this remit we cannot tell. It was certainly never submitted to the special Commission appointed to deal with it, and Scot of Cupar (himself a member) doubted if any such book had been drawn up ' by those to whom it was committed.' But it seems from the proceedings of the Privy Council in 1618 that a draft had been before the Perth Assembly of that year.

It would appear, therefore, that at the time of the accession of Charles, two similar or dissimilar schemes were in existence for the drawing nearer of the two Churches, one with both its feet planted in the Scottish tradition, and the other the work of a dominant spirit outside that tradition.

It would be quite impossible within the limits of this paper to recount the whole story of the negotiations which ended in the imposition of the Canons of 1636 and the Liturgy of 1637 ; its special purpose is to examine certain current conceptions of the part played in them by Laud and to lay bare, if possible, the motives which animated him throughout.

Dr. Cooper, among many others, will have it that Laud's Liturgy is a misnomer, and that the responsibility or the credit for that production belongs to the younger Scottish bishops. He accepts Laud's apologetic reconstruction throughout and particularly his claim that he had ' laboured to have the English Liturgy sent ' to the Scots ' without any omission or addition at all,' and that ' some of the Scottish bishops prevailed herein ' against him. It is remarkable that Laud does not attempt to evade responsibility for the Canons, which have attracted fewer defenders than the Liturgy. In their case he admits that the Scottish Church had made a sound beginning, that the Bishop of Ross brought a copy [1] to him, with blank pages for corrections and additions, and that he had to put all in better order, which was no censurable crime. ' And whatever they of Scotland think, that Church did then need many things to be put in better order, and at this day need many more.' He admitted, further, that he had added one Canon at the last moment, that he had definitely changed some others as out of harmony with the teaching and practice of Church of England, and that the 4th Canon of Chapter VIII did ' stand behind the curtain,' and is ' to be printed fully, as one that was to be most useful.' He admitted finally that he had changed the title from ' Canons agreed to be proponed to Synods,' to Canons ' ordained to be observed by the Clergy,' endeavouring, however, to explain away the implications of this change. That is to say, he defends the Canons as originally of Scottish provenance, but soundly revised and supplemented by himself and the Bishop of London; and does not even wholly evade responsibility for the method of their introduction.

As for the Liturgy, however, his claim was that he wanted the English one as it stood ; it was the Scottish prelates who were responsible for any change, imply-

---

[1] It is evident that these draft Canons were not compiled according to the formula of the General Assembly of 1616 ; even in their first draft they must have borne a closer relation to the English Canons of 1604 than to excerpts from Acts of General Assemblies.

ing thereby the specific changes which had roused
the people. What plausibility there is in this statement
comes from the suppression of material facts. Laud
gives no hint anywhere that, when Bishop Maxwell
visited him, he came with the Liturgy prepared con-
temporaneously with the Canons, brought up to date
as its prayer for the Royal family proves. It was for
this amended version of Knox's Liturgy that the Scottish
bishops sought the approval of Charles, certain that it
would have had the benediction of his father.[1] It was
then that Laud persuaded the King to insist on the
English Liturgy, as much preferable to these meagre
and beggarly rudiments. At that time the Scottish
bishops intimated that they, on their part, were not
prepared to go further than they had gone.

For four years matters were at a standstill. Then
came, in 1633, the visit of Charles I to Scotland for his
coronation, with Laud as his ecclesiastical adviser and
master of ceremonies. From the meagre notes in his
diary we gather that he came to regard the very
country with aversion, e.g. 'July 8, Monday [from
Perth] to Dumblain and Stirling, my dangerous and
cruel journey crossing part of the Hilands by Coach,
which was a wonder there.'

It is evident that during this visit Laud had many
talks with the Scottish bishops, in which the latter
made it clear ' that they would be better pleased to
have a Liturgie of their own, but such as should come
near the English both in Form and Matter.' That

[1] In a paper drawn up by the Earl of Stirling it is related that ' this
very book *in statu quo* King James left it, was sent to his Majesty
and presented to his Majesty by myself (whether the same was done
or not by the Bishop of Ross, I dare not confidently averre, but I think
hee it was).'

is to say they requested in effect that they should be allowed to take their own production as a basis, and make some further amendments on it. To this request both Charles and Laud refused to listen ; and on their return to England, Laud began his campaign in the King's name. Pending a final settlement, the use of the English Liturgy was to be extended in Scotland. It had already been observed, at least in part, in the Chapel Royal at Holyrood ; henceforward it was to be used without deviation or diminution ; attendance there once a year at a full Anglican Communion was enjoined on an enlarging circle of those in official positions in Scotland. Non-conforming officials were to be punished. Finally, in October 1634, its use was enjoined in ' Cathedral Churches on all holydays,' and twice a day in all Episcopal households.

Laud's great trouble in this business was to find willing agents. Spottiswoode, the Primate and Chancellor, proved a broken reed : he was too deeply attached to the Scottish tradition ; Bellenden, Dean of the Chapel Royal, was the recipient of more than one sharp reminder that promotion depended on his full obedience. ' His Majesty commanded me to write expressly to you, that he did not take it well that, contrary to his express command, you had omitted prayers in his Chappell Royall, according to the English Litturgye ; with some other omissions there, which pleased him not ' ; the only fairly reliable ally was Bishop Maxwell of Ross. Up to the time of the promulgation of the Canons, Maxwell showed himself all that Laud could desire in a Scottish colleague. Even when the first amendments to the English Liturgy proved to be completely away from the Scottish direction, he was still amenable. But it is evident that there were changes which stuck in his throat. So Laud had to fall back on his solitary whole-hearted supporter, that James Wedderburn, who, having spent over twelve years in Laudian circles in England, was sent back to Scotland in 1635 as Bishop of Dunblane and Dean of the Chapel Royal. Laud commended him to Bishop Maxwell as ' very able to do service and will certainly do it, if you can keep up his heart,' showing already how conscious he was that Wedderburn would find himself depressed by lack of support. As Dean he had instructions to stickle at nothing, and was assured that the King would reward fervent loyalty with quick promotion. In him Laud had an agent entirely to his mind. Baillie calls him ' a man sett in the Chappell to be a hand to Canterburie in all his intentions.' The correspondence between the two reveals their essential kinship. The significant details at which Maxwell scrupled rejoiced the heart of Wedderburn. Hence the final instructions about the printing of the Liturgy ran thus : ' So in the printing of your Liturgy you are to follow the book which my Lord Ross brought, *and the additions* which are made to the book I now send. But if you find the book of my Lord Ross's, and this, to differ in anything that is material, there you are to follow this later book I now send, as expressing some things more fully.' In his elaborate defence, Laud claimed that he was not responsible for the method of introducing the book—by royal mandate—that, on the contrary, he had left the Scottish prelates to do so according to the laws and customs of their Church. And yet this same letter to Wedderburn contains this final paragraph : ' In His Majesty's authorising of the notes in this book prefixed at the beginning of it, though he leave a liberty to my Lord the Archbishop of St. Andrewes, and brethren the Bishops who are upon the place, upon apparent reason to vary some things ; yet you must know, and inform them, that His Majesty having viewed all these additions, hopes that there will be no need of change of anything, and will be best pleased with little or rather no alteration.'

Thus the final form of the Liturgy would come as a surprise even to the Bishop of Ross. Canterbury and Dunblane—with the possible exceptions of King Charles and Bishop Wren—were the only two who knew precisely what to expect. There is no evading the conclusion that Laud used Wedderburn to revise the English Liturgy in a ritualistic direction, endeavouring to get behind the Elizabethan Compromise to the First Prayer-book of King Edward VI, and in points, behind even that, to mediæval practice. ' These variations were taken, either from the first book of Edward VI, which was not popery ; or from some ancient Liturgies which savoured not of popery.'

Was there, then, no attempt to meet genuine Scottish wishes ? Apart from the partial but incomplete discarding of lessons from the Apocrypha, I can find no trace of any. The one that is constantly cited is the substitution of Presbyter for Priest throughout. Before this is accepted, a closer scrutiny must be given to the actual changes made in the current Prayer-book of England, that of 1604. Priest is not the uniform name for the officiating clergyman in that book. It is used, it is true, fifty-five times, and is always, in the Scottish Liturgy, replaced by Presbyter. But the word Minister is used ninety-two times, and it is replaced fifty-three times by Presbyter, and thirty-nine times by Presbyter or Minister. Quite evidently Laud had seized the opportunity afforded by the Scottish dislike of the name Priest, to get rid of that other name so favoured by the Puritans, and therefore so obnoxious to his ears, ' Minister.' And to one of his school of thought it mattered little whether the displacing word was ' Presbyter ' or ' Priest.' To him, as to Milton, though for a different reason, Presbyter was but Priest writ large. I cannot find a single expression in the book that Laud would not have been willing to sponsor for England.

Next, it is to be noted that although Laud, in view of the disastrous failure of the book in Scotland, made an elaborate attempt to shift the responsibility on to Scottish shoulders, he never attempted to conceal his admiration for what he was pleased to call *their* work. One of the last tasks that he undertook was a translation of it into Latin, prepared in order that the learned world throughout Europe might fully appreciate its quality. He upheld it, on every point, and at times with cogency and pungency against every definite Scottish challenge. Here are some of his pronouncements : ' I like the book exceedingly well, and hope I shall be able to maintain anything that is in it.' ' That Kingdom (has lost) such a form of God's service, as I fear they will never come near again.' ' Though I shall not find fault with the order of the prayers, as they stand in the Communion-book of England (for, God be thanked, 'tis well) ; yet, if a comparison must be made, I do think the order of the prayers, as now they stand in the Scottish Liturgy, to be the better, and more agreeable to use in the primitive Church.'

' 'Tis true, this passage is not in the Prayer of Consecration in the Service-book of England ; but I wish with all my heart it were. For though the consecration of the elements may be without it, yet it is much more solemn and full be that invocation.' ' As for " the oblation of the elements," that is fit and proper ; and I am sorry, for my part, that it is not in the Book of England.' He makes it clear that, while disclaiming authorship, he is prepared to defend every jot and tittle of the alterations on the merits. This is even more evident in the ' side-papers ' to Strafford, to which reference has already been made. Here the Liturgy is referred to as the ' *summum bonum*,' containing some differences from the English, and 'those well-weighed.' ' It troubles me too, and I believe as much as any man, that that which might have been *summum bonum* hath been so shamelessly lost in 197 (Scotland), and we are now glad of *minus malum*, which is the choice which necessity allows and no better.' No more need be adduced to prove that Laud thought of the Scottish Liturgy (however reluctant he was to admit any real share in its preparation) as the best conceivable liturgy for that day and generation.

Now, where does all this lead? Can we believe that Laud, having seen a *summum bonum* set up in Scotland, was going to rest content with a *minus bonum* for England? Can we believe that England was not Laud's main objective? Recall his situation. Labouring incessantly for certain reforms of worship in England, he is hampered at every turn by recalcitrants challenging the adequacy of his authority for them. In the heat of parties in England, with so many still Abbott's men, there is no chance of Canons or Liturgy being amended to Laud's

mind. Nor can he dare to stretch the Royal prerogative any further. Is there any way out? Did
Laud in this dilemma see a glimmer of hope by way
of Scotland? Did he recall these words of King
James at St. Andrews about the 'power belonging to
all Christian princes to order matters in the Church'?
Could not the Church of Scotland be reformed by this
method, and then a loud call to Uniformity with this
remodelled Scottish Church become the slogan of his
party? This is the one explanation that seems to fit
all the facts. It gives the canon which 'stands behind
the curtain' its function 'as one that was to be most
useful.' What worried Scotsmen about this canon was
that it took all initiative and power from the Courts
of the Church, and left the King free to bring in what
innovations he chose; what pleased Laud about it
was that, once Canons and Liturgy had been established by that power to order matters in the Church
which belonged to the Christian prince, no alteration
of any kind could be made apart from him. 'Forasmuch,' it runs, 'as no reformation in doctrine or discipline can be made perfect at once in any Church,
therefore it shall and may be lawful for the Church of
Scotland at any time to make remonstrance to His
Majesty, or his successors, what they conceive fit to be
taken in further consideration in and concerning the
premises. And if the King shall thereupon declare his
liking and approbation, then both clergy and lay shall
yield their obedience, without incurring the censure
aforesaid or any other. But it shall not be lawful for
the bishops themselves, in a national synod or other-
wise, to alter any rubric, article, canon, doctrinal or
disciplinary, whatsoever, under the pain above men-

tioned, and His Majesty's further displeasure.' With this canon once accepted, the Liturgy of his dreams might be established and stabilized in Scotland; England, impressed by the sheer merit of that Liturgy, could easily be induced to conform. Most historians, in concentrating on Laud's conceivable aims for Scotland, have lost sight of his ultimate aim. Scotland only came into the picture at all as a possible strategic base for ending the deadlock in England, and bringing victory to his hard-pressed henchmen.

It may be asked, why has this reading of Laud's intervention in Scotland not been suggested before? The answer is that it was, though the fact seems to have been overlooked. The Scottish Commissioners who brought the original charges against Laud, through Adam Blair their clerk, transmitted to the English Parliament a supplementary list in which the English prelates in general were conjoined with Laud. A main part of this second document reads thus : ' It hath come to pass of late, that the prelates of England having prevailed and brought us to subjection in point of government, and finding their long-waited-for opportunity and a rare congruity of many spirits and powers ready to co-operate for their ends, have made a strong assault upon the whole external worship and doctrine of our Kirk. By this their doing they did not aim to make us conform to England but to make Scotland first (whose weakness in resisting they had before experienced in novations of government and of some points of worship), and thereafter England, conform to Rome, even in those matters wherein England had separated from Rome ever since the time of Reformation.' In his answer, Laud naturally fastens on the phrase ' conform to Rome,' which he asserts is a manifest and ' monstrous untruth,' ' considering what the Bishops of England have written in defence of their Reformation against Rome, and how far beyond anything which the presybters of Scotland have written against it.' But if the Scottish Commissioners had avoided this unfortunate phrase and said ' return to mediæval practice even in points deliberately discarded at the Reformation,' Laud would have found himself hard put to it to find any answer. Indeed, had he not been a prisoner in danger of his life, I do not think he would have attempted an answer. He would have acknowledged the justice of the charge, and gloried in it, lamenting only the failure of the plan. *Summum bonum* for England—the restoration of priestly rites and ancient values—was to come through that *summum bonum* attained in Scotland. It is the wreckage of this great scheme that explains Laud's bitter exasperation with the Scots. It was not that by their determined obstinacy they had missed a good thing for themselves ; they had ruined the golden dream for England which it was his dearest ambition to achieve.

The elements in the resistance which the fateful plan encountered have often been analysed. There was the selfish fear of not a few, resenting the royal plans for restitution of some of the ancient patrimony ; there was an early stirring of Scottish nationalism, lamenting the unexpected results of the transference of the Scottish Royal line to the southern capital ; there was a notable recrudescence of Presbyterian fervour, suppressed and driven into the solitudes for well-nigh a generation. But neither selfish, nor patriotic, nor ecclesiastical interests—no, nor all combined—can account for the quality of that resistance. Fundamentally it was religious. It was a definite concern for the gains of the Reformation, and at the heart of it, for one particular element in that gain. This was the elevation of the Lord's Supper in its simplicities to be the spiritual sustenance of the believing community. 'We affirme,' says the Scots Confession, 'that the faithfull in the rycht use of the Lordis Table hes sick conjunctioun with Christ Jesus, as the naturall man can not comprehend.' And teachers like Robert Bruce had led the common man at the Table to know his Redeemer near and his redemption sure. It is this that has led Lord Eustace Percy to label the Scottish Church as 'in the strict sense of the term, a Eucharistic Church.' In England, many had thought that if they took the Mass, and washed its face, and taught it English, it could be received into good society ; in Scotland, it was the irredeemable degradation of the Sacrament in the Mass that moved the Lords of the Congregation. 'Secondlie,' so ran their official supplication to the Parliament of 1560, 'seing that the Sacramentis of Jesus Chryst are maist schamefullie abusit and prophanit by that Romane harlot and hir sworne vassallis.' A fully restored Sacrament, in which, as they conceived it, no tradition of man was to be found, had, for three generations, been the living nerve and centre of Scottish religion. And now, here was Laud, with his altar, and a Presbyter turning his back on the people, and mumbling prayers, and using old formulæ in translation ! Whether the words were ever spoken or not, the traditional 'Fause loon, dost thou daur say Mass at ma lug,' fitly sums up the

Scottish feeling. This was the road back to Rome. It was to imperil all that had been won. And while liturgists may defend everything in word and rubric in the Communion Service of the Prayer-book of 1637 as sound and traditional and admirable, I hold that the Scottish Church would have lost infinitely more by its acceptance than they might conceivably have gained.

Laud never knew the extent of his offence. His was a one-track mind. He could enter into no tradition save his own ; and, all unwittingly, he had threatened another tradition, prized beyond price by a host of believing souls, and already deeply embedded in the heart of a people. Hence Scotland, as a base of operations for a decisive victory in a divided England, proved a delusion and a snare ; and his attempt to establish it sealed his doom.

SOLEMN LEAGUE AND COVENANT

17TH AUGUST 1643 was one of the most jubilant days
in the history of the Scottish capital. It saw the first
production of the text of the Solemn League and
Covenant before two bodies, the General Assembly
and the Convention of Estates. In the forenoon, in
the General Assembly, it was introduced by Alexander
Henderson, Moderator for the third time in five years,
in a 'most grave oration'; thereafter it was twice
read by him slowly and distinctly, and adopted, after
some prominent ministers and elders had expressed
their warm approval, without a dissentient voice.
Robert Baillie records that 'it was received with
the greatest applause that ever I saw anything,
with so hearty affections, expressed in the tears of
pity and joy by very many grave, wise, and old
men.'

Its reception in the afternoon in the Convention of
Estates was marked by an enthusiasm reflected in the
text of the proceedings ; it stands written in the official
record of the Scottish Parliament : ' We, Noblemen,
Commissioners of Shires and burghs, now convened,
having received the Covenant above-written . . . did
with all their hearts and great expressions of joy and
unanimity approve and embrace the same as the most
powerful means by the blessing of God for settling and
preserving the true protestant religion with a perfect
peace in all His Majesty's dominions and propagating

the same to other nations, and for establishing His Majesty's throne to all ages.'

It is difficult for us who know the events of the immediately succeeding period—the grim battles of the Civil War both in England and Scotland, the imprisonment and execution of the King, the unwelcome interventions of the Protector, the Restoration of the Stuart line with the generation of proscription and persecution that followed—to understand the jubilation and the haste.

On the surface, all the jubilation should have been in London, at the headquarters of the Parliament. In a season of desperate crisis, when a crushing defeat seemed at least a possibility, they had, in the very nick of time, secured the intervention of a Scottish army. Neither in money nor in conditions was the price extortionate. They had angled for a civil league only, and, while a religious covenant was a novelty, it did not commit them to anything beyond the policy on which they had already embarked. Laud's Episcopacy had gone, and they had set up the Westminster Assembly to lay down the lines of the new ecclesiastical order. They had no desire to disturb the religious settlement of Scotland : they were ready to guarantee its stability ; and a Reformation in England to bring it into line with the best Reformed Churches was their own declared aim. If Scotland also was ready, for the sake of uniformity and stability, to accept the work of their constituted Assembly with some leading Scots present in an advisory capacity, this was all to the good. Haste and jubilation in London are intelligible, but why in Edinburgh ?

The treaty of 1641, after the Second Bishops' War,

had granted the Scottish Covenanters all their demands. The National Covenant had, within three and a half years, accomplished its work. The Presbyterian settlement appeared secure. Clouds had gathered with the outbreak of Civil War in England. The Cavalier and Roundhead cleavage began to show signs of spreading into Scotland. Was Scotland to remain neutral in the struggle? Both sides appealed for Scottish support. Scotland's first instinct was to mediate, and more than one promising, but abortive, attempt was made. From these it appeared that Charles was in the grip of advisers as hostile to the Scottish Church as ever were Strafford and Laud. In the event of a Royal victory, was the Scottish settlement safe? It never seems to have entered their minds that, in the event of a Parliamentary victory, the King might not be safe. They seem to have anticipated the same kind of result as from victory in a general election—the King on the throne with a completely new set of advisers.

So the prospect of a deputation from the English Parliament and the Westminster Assembly with full powers of negotiation was welcomed equally by the General Assembly and the Convention of Estates, special meetings of both being summoned. The Assembly met on 2nd August, expecting that Sir Harry Vane and his fellow-commissioners would already have arrived. Days passed with no word of them, and the Assembly had to spin out routine business to an inordinate length. The six delegates did not land at Leith until Monday, the 7th, and presented their credentials to the Assembly on the 8th. Their business was entered on without delay. A committee of the General Assembly and one of the Convention of Estates met with them daily. At first the going was hard. There was unanimity as to giving aid to the Parliament by the dispatch of Scottish troops to England. But in what capacity? Robert Baillie, who was a member, tells us: ' One night all were bent to go as Redders, and friends to both, without siding altogether with the Parliament.' It was not an Englishman, but a Scot, who demonstrated the futility of this fond dream. So, gradually, solid identification with the side of the Parliament became the unanimous mind and, on the basis of a draft submitted by Henderson, the Solemn League and Covenant was hammered into shape by the committee, to be adopted with acclamation by the parent bodies.

It had no validity, of course, until the English Parliament had approved it. This was done in September, with some slight amendments in the wording. Public subscription began on 25th September. A gathering of representative men in St. Margaret's, Westminster, with uplifted hands swore to the Covenant, and appended their names. The corresponding day in Scotland was Friday, 13th October, when, within St. Giles 'in the new Church,' after an address by Robert Douglas, signing began. On 19th January 1644, the Earl of Leven began to cross the Tweed at the head of an army of 21,000 men. The Westminster Assembly had turned in October from revision of doctrine to the more pressing questions of polity and worship. The first-fruits of the Solemn League and Covenant were all that could be desired. No one could have dreamt that to the next in the list of the rulers of Scotland it would savour of a Covenant with death and an agreement with hell; and that under the next but one it would be publicly torn to pieces in Edinburgh by the hangman, and its adherents hunted and harried on the hills ; nor that to many English minds, and not the least enlightened, it would become a synonym for intolerance and bigotry.

There is no doubt that in many parts of England it was made an inexorable instrument of constriction, but was this inherent in the Covenant as such ? Had Henderson and the rest of them plausible reason to believe that it would be welcomed in England without any ' forcing of conscience,' and that they might safely leave the working of their vision of unity to the decision of English Divines ? We must recall that they had spent some months of 1641 in London ; that they had been hailed as saviours of the English situation ; that they had preached to crowds who, despite their ' barbarous accents,' hung upon their words; that in every quarter they had been asked to explain every detail of their Scottish system ; that they were living in the London of the Root and Branch Petition, a London which, in its reaction from rampant Prelacy, seemed to have become rampageously Presbyterian. They had every reason to think that they were bringing nothing but deliverance to an oppressed people. The documents which the English Divines ultimately produced, and the actions of the citizens of London in their support, indicate that their belief was not ill-founded.

But they forgot that London was not England and that the Divines they met were not an average sample of the English clergy, and that what was liberation to the like-minded was liable to become, through Parliamentary enforcements, to others an insufferable bondage.

Two of our greatest poets have been moved to give their verdict on the Solemn League and Covenant. To the Scot, Robert Burns, 'it sealed freedom's noble cause.' To the Englishman, John Milton, it brought in the civil sword ' to force our consciences that Christ set free.' Even the best devised instrument can be wrongly handled.

THE COVENANTS IN EIGHTEENTH-CENTURY SCOTLAND

No phase of our Scottish religion has given greater sport to the Philistines than the renewal of the Covenants. To those who disapproved of these documents altogether it was a pathetic exhibition of futility. Whatever excuse there was for the plain disloyalty of the original action in the reign of a coercive Stuart, to revive them under the harmless Hanoverians only served to demonstrate the ineradicable disloyalty of an intransigent Scottish minority, unhinged by a grandiose dream of Presbyterian supremacy. Even those who looked back on the Covenants with pride and affection thought and spoke of their renewal as an impossible attempt to recover the heroism and the glories of a long-vanished past—a miserable anachronism perpetrated by an insignificant remnant. The few to-day outside Scotland who have ever heard of the practice, regard it as an unintelligible exercise associated with a place with an unpronounceable name—Auchensaugh—and a body with incomprehensible tenets—the Cameronians. And every student of Scottish religion who has any familiarity with the meaning and text of the Covenants must be impressed with the folly of any sectional interest within the nation proposing, in any effective sense, to renew the vows and pledges of 1638 and 1643. No more remote and unpromising subject could, it would appear, be proposed for investigation.

But every now and then, in the reminiscences of churchmen born within the eighteenth century—not reared in the protesting remnant of the Cameronians—one is brought up against this surprising fact that they assign a conspicuous place in their own spiritual development to some public ceremonial which they call a renewal of the Covenants. It is to be found most frequently among those brought up within the fellowship of the Seceders, but it is not absent from the experiences of others whose spiritual home was the main body of the Church of Scotland in its more Evangelical circles. It becomes apparent that renewal of the Covenants must mean something other than the words themselves convey, that the engagement of mind and heart was not simply with the past, and that for those who took part, it involved a soul-stirring and life-renovating upturn in the actual present.

The search for a clue to this problem leads into unexpected regions, both geographically and religiously. While it may be hard to disentangle the history of the various developments, and to appreciate the motives behind them, the story that emerges is worthy of reconstruction, is not so remote and unpromising as it sounds, and lays bare one nerve of eighteenth-century piety.

The story has its beginning in the Revolution Settlement of 1689. As is well known, that settlement was based on the earlier one of a century before—the Charter of the Church of 1592. While the worst Acts of the second Covenanting period were expressly rescinded, there was no mention of the Covenants. They were simply ignored. Now to the Society people who had followed Richard Cameron this was a gross defection from the testimony of the martyrs, and rank disloyalty both to their fathers who had joined themselves in a perpetual Covenant with God and to the God to whom they had then as a nation bound themselves. Could a nation which accepted the restoration of the Presbyterian Church merely on the score of its acceptability to the general inclinations of the people, and which gave its allegiance to a king who, once a Presbyterian, was now as tainted with Episcopacy as those predecessors of his whom it had explicitly disowned, be called in any sense a Covenanted nation? While their ministers entered the Church of the Settlement, tabling their protests as they came, the elders and members of the organized Societies refused to desert the principles to which, in 1681 on the lonely moors near Logan House, they had pledged their allegiance. They stood by the Covenants in their entirety. They were the faithful remnant of God's loyal people ; and He would not forsake His own. They issued testimony after testimony, from which it appeared that their consciences would not allow them to regard the Covenants as an emergency expedient, but as of perpetual obligation.

Their Covenanting fervour grew as they saw the Church of Scotland accept, always under protest, one encroachment after another on its high claim to freedom. The Union of 1707 increased their concern, but what constituted the final proof of national defection was the legislation of 1712. When by two Acts of the British Parliament the yoke of Patronage was reimposed and authorization given to the use of the Anglican Liturgy in Scotland, what was to the Church of Scotland a breach of faith against which no words of protest were too strong, was to them a call to action. Now was the time to renew the Covenants—to demonstrate to the world that there were some in Scotland whose protest was manifest in deeds as well as words.

In prosecution of this end, messages were sent to all the Societies to come in as full numbers as possible to a central spot—the lonely heights of Auchensaugh, near Douglas, in the Upper Ward of Lanarkshire—in readiness for a Mass Meeting which was to last several days, beginning on the 23rd of July 1712. And so, in the pause before the late upland hay-time, cottars and farmers with a small sprinkling of professional men and lesser lairds from all over the south of Scotland —from the Mull of Galloway to the outskirts of Edinburgh—began to converge on the set day at the appointed site, bringing with them such food and shelter as they could. For three days the solemnities continued, as the delegates to the last General Meeting had determined. The main concern of the first day was what must have been a very long sermon by the Rev. John McNeile, a licentiate of the Church of Scotland, who had cast in his lot with the Societies. He was not, however (such was their reverence for Presbyterian order), regarded at that time as a minister in full status, though he was given complete liberty in that which he had been licensed to do—to preach the Gospel. His text was Jer. 50 : 4 and 5 : 'In those days, and in that time, saith the Lord, the children of Israel shall come, they and the children of Judah together, going and weeping. . . . They shall ask the way to Zion with their faces thitherward, saying, Come, and let us join ourselves unto the Lord, in a perpetual covenant that shall not be forgotten.' To the gathered ranks of the like-minded who had never seen each other face to face before, and who were prepared in some measure to equate the Scottish Covenants with God's Covenant with Israel, it must have been a most powerful discourse, never to be forgotten. At the close of the sermon the prepared documents were solemnly read. These were slightly revised versions of the two historic Covenants, followed by a formal pledge ; an Acknowledgement of Sins consisting of a detailed catalogue of breaches of the Covenants on the part of themselves individually and of the corporate nation ; and what was called an Engagement to Duties. On the 24th, their solitary ordained minister, Rev. John MacMillan, formerly of Balmaghie, preached with at least equal fervour, if not at equal length, on Isaiah 44 : 5 : 'One shall say, I am the Lord's ; and another shall call himself by the name of Jacob ; and another shall subscribe with his hand unto the Lord, and surname himself by the name of Israel.' An equally moving sermon in all the circumstances of the gathering, it creates the impression on a reader of to-day of fervid *Scottish-Israelitism*. Its central point is in the third remark under the third head. ' A Right Covenanter must be well resolved concerning the Terms of the Covenant : that it excludes all coming and going, according to the Revolutions of the Times, and the Ebbing and Flowing of Worldly Interests : One that has given up His Name to the Lord in Covenant, and called himself by the Name of Israel must not, like the *Samaritans* be an *Israelite* only in the time of *Israel's* prosperity, but he must be one in adversity too. The things engaged to in the Covenant being of an Everlasting and Permanent Duration in their Nature, must be lasting also in their Observation.' After the sermon the documents were again produced, and immediately after the Acknowledgement of Sins had been read for the second time, Mr. MacMillan called upon all those who were conscious of being involved in any way in these defections to make public avowal of these their sins, setting the example by a notable confession of his own public failures in entire loyalty to the Covenants. A Communion Service was to follow, whether on the next day or not is not clear from the contemporary narrative, and no one was to be admitted to the Table who had not thus renewed the Covenants. So far as can be gathered, no one was missing from the celebration, for many of them their first Lord's Supper in twenty years.

Certain questions concerning the whole transaction demand an answer at this point. The first is, what was the nature of the amendments introduced into the text of the Covenants? The main one was that the references to loyalty to the King's Majesty, his person, and his authority had to be amended—not simply, as in the current Prayer-books, by the substitution of Queen for King. While ' Lawful supreme magistrate ' is the normal substitute, sometimes it is more explicit : ' The Persons and Authority of Sovereigns, having the Qualifications which the Scriptures require.' Then all references to corruptions in the Church had to be brought up to date by insertions like these, ' or any other Corruptions thereof, Prelatic or Erastian, either tryed or to be tryed, such as Indulgence, the Toleration, the Magistrates appointing Fasts without Advice and Consent of the Church, Dissolving Assemblies, etc.' The Solemn League and Covenant presented one

special crux with its reference to the endeavour that
' the two Parliaments may be and remain conjoined
in a firm Peace and Union to all Posterity.' These
strenuous opponents of the Union of 1707 got round
it by inserting after ' Parliaments ' the words ' as they
were then.' But the changes are not formidable in
bulk, nor surprising in content.

The second question is, what was the exact formula
under which they subscribed the amended Covenants ?
It ran thus : ' These Covenants above written, formerly
nationally taken and renewed, and still nationally
binding, We, in our private Station only, swear and
subscribe in their genuine sense, conform to the Explication and Application thereof in our Present
Acknowledgement of the Public Sins and Breaches of
the Same, and our Engagement to the Duties contained
therein, which do in a special way relate to the present
Times, and are proper for our Capacities therein.' In
how far the words, ' in their genuine sense,' were
modified in the minds of these renewers of the Covenant
by the proviso that followed, ' conform to the explication and application thereof,' will appear from the
contents of the two papers which incorporate this
explication and application.

The *Solemn Acknowledgement of Publick Sins, and
Breaches of the National Covenant and Solemn League and
Covenant* demands more than 20,000 words for its
unfolding. Modelled on an earlier one of 1649 at
the height of the Resolutioner-Protester controversy,
its purport is plain from this paragraph : ' We do
humbly and sincerely, as in His sight who is the
searcher of hearts, acknowledge the many sins and
great transgressions of the land : We have done

wickedly, our Kings, our Princes, our Nobles, our Judges, our Officers, our Teachers, and our People. Albeit the Lord hath long and clearly spoken unto us, we have not hearkened to His voice. Albeit He hath followed us with tender mercies, we have not been allured to wait upon Him and to walk in His way. And though He hath stricken us, yet we have not grieved ; Nay, though He hath consumed us, we have refused to receive Correction. We have not remembered to render unto the Lord according to His goodness, and according to our vows and promises ; but have gone backwards by a perpetual backsliding, and have most sinfully and shamefully broken the National Covenant, and all the articles of the Solemn League and Covenant, which our fathers sware before God, angels, and men.' Then follows an exhaustive enumeration of the offences past and present, interspersed with fine, but rather irrelevant, quotations from both the Old Testament and the New. Naturally special stress is laid upon the support and toleration of Prelacy, and the Erastian encroachments on the freedom of the Church. But they have a wider range than this. How some of the tabulated offences, however reprehensible, could be regarded as breaches of the Solemn League and Covenant is hard to see. Here are some of the surprising entries : 'the Liberty allowed (by the State) to that pestilential generation of Quakers, who keep their General Meetings yearly in Edinburgh, being guarded by a company of the Town Guards ' : ' some using the Lord's Prayer *as a set-form*, which ought to be used as a rule of direction in all our prayers, and not *as a dead form of words*': profanations of the Holy Sabbath such as ' Sounding trumpets before the Lords of Justiciary when going to Church': and the defects in the national administration of justice, 'Witness the frequent *indemnities* and *remissions* granted to murderers; as particularly, the passing without punishment the Persons which perpetrate that inhumane, Barbarous, and Lawless Action of the Massacre of Glencoe.'

The *Solemn Engagement* is naturally shorter. It particularizes the duties incumbent on those who would stem this course of defection. The distinctive note is sounded in dealing with their civil allegiance to an uncovenanted Government. 'Albeit God, in His righteous judgment, hath left the Nations so far to the counsels of their own hearts . . . as to give up the rights and privileges of Parliament and Kingdom to the will and lust of the *English*, and so to betray the interest both of Religion and Civil Liberty for unworthy by-ends; yet we purpose and promise that we shall always in our capacities bear witness against these courses, and shall not by any means corroborate them, or encourage and countenance the maintainers and abettors of them.' But 'bearing witness against these courses' was not enough; they engaged themselves not to uphold the present régime 'by paying them Cess and Supply for upholding their corrupt courts and armies employed in an unjust and Antichristian quarrel (*i.e.* the campaigns of Marlborough) or by compearing before their Judicatories, either to defend or pursue law-suits, or upon any other account.'

Most of the other engagements might have been taken by the most loyal member of the Church of Scotland, who would have been whole-heartedly with them in their final pledge: 'Therefore, denying ourselves and our own things, and laying aside all self-interests and ends, we shall, above all things, seek the honour of God, the good of His Cause, and the Wealth (*i.e.* weal) of His people ; and that, forsaking the counsels of flesh and blood, and not leaning upon Carnal Confidences, we shall depend upon the Lord ; walk by the rule of His word ; and hearken to the voice of His servants.'

It will be evident from this brief and unbiassed account of what was transacted at Auchensaugh that we are in contact here with something that can legitimately be called a 'renewal of the Covenants.' Amendments and explanations notwithstanding, the historic Covenants dominate everything that was said and done. While, as is evident from stray fragments of biography, individual members of the assembled crowds felt that they had publicly renewed their personal Covenant with God, the dominant feeling was that, according to their capacity as an organized minority, they had placed themselves alongside the fathers who had pledged themselves in the same Covenants as constituent elements of a more or less united nation. They would not rest content till all the imagined glories of the Golden Age of the 1640's were theirs once more ; nor would they recognize any Government which acquiesced in less.

Their removal of all reference to the King's Majesty from the text of the Covenant lent credibility to the charge of Kerr of Kersland that they favoured the Pretender and were ready to take up arms on his behalf. No accusation could have been more wide of the mark. To any genuine Cameronian this would have been like disowning the Archbishop of Canterbury to enthrone the Pope. Though there was no satisfactory alternative within the whole horizon, God would, in His own time and way, grant to a penitent and praying people ' a sovereign having the qualifications which the Scriptures require.'

While Auchensaugh is the outstanding example of this type of renewal of the Covenants, it was repeated on a lesser scale by the Reformed Presbyterians on many occasions during the eighteenth century, normally with a revised version of the sins to be acknowledged and the particular engagements to be undertaken ; and when, through emigration and missionary activity, they established Churches overseas, this renewal of the Covenants remained a term of communion. Periodical gatherings for this purpose were a prominent feature of their Churches in Ireland, which may have helped to account for the use or abuse of the name Covenanter in the days preceding the last war.

What is perhaps of greater interest and significance is that Auchensaugh was re-enacted in America at Middle Octarara in Pennsylvania almost a generation later, on 11th November 1743. On that day there was a considerable gathering in the open ; the Covenants were read exactly as amended for Auchensaugh ; a sermon was preached on the same text, and with practically the same contents ; and there was a similar but much shorter Acknowledgement of Sins, followed by a Solemn Engagement, much more bluntly expressed. Here, for example, is the one relating to civil authority, corresponding to the earlier one quoted above. ' We look upon it as our duty to separate ourselves from the corrupt constitution of both Church and State, and not to touch, taste, nor handle these abominations, lest by partaking with them in their sins, we be made

77

partakers with them in their plagues.' The brevity
of the Acknowledgement of Sins is explained when we
find incorporated an extra document which covers
much of the ground. It is entitled ' The Declaration,
Protestation, and Testimony of a suffering Remnant
of the Anti-Popish, Anti-Lutherian, Anti-Prelatick,
Anti-Erastian, Anti-Latitudinarian, Anti-Sectarian, true
Presbyterian Church in America.' This title outdoes
the best efforts of their Scottish confrères ; and the
contents correspond. Here, for example, is the reference to William III (though at the first glance it might
be read as a protest against some local intruder into
the Pennsylvanian ministry). ' We likewise state our
testimony against the instalment of *William Henry*,
because he had neither national nor scriptural qualifications, but exactly contrary thereunto.'

It was but a tiny ripple that this somewhat feeble
aping of its Scottish prototype created in American
waters, and the strenuous efforts of Mr. Craighead, its
organizer, to have Octarara repeated in other centres
on a wider scale seem to have been hardly adequate
to keep the ripple visible. Yet it may be that it was
not without its effects—in two directions. Had these
early gatherings in the open no part to play in shaping
the course of the Camp Meeting revivals which meant
so much for the development of religion in the Colonies;
and did this open renunciation of uncovenanted British
rulers provide no preparation for the repudiation of
British rule altogether in the Declaration of Independence ? The participants were conscious of neither
aim, but gatherings like these may put forth longer
tentacles than their organizers planned.

Had these somewhat picturesque but futile efforts of

the Cameronians to recreate a vanished past been the only episodes that took the name of Renewals of the Covenants, the whole subject might be permitted to fall into oblivion. But within two months of the first of the American ventures at Octarara, a new series had been initiated in Scotland by the adolescent Seceders, in total ignorance of what had happened across the Atlantic. Almost the first Act of the Associate Presbytery was to issue a Testimony against the defections of the Church of Scotland which had reference mainly to its recent defections, particularly in regard to its acquiescence in Patronage and its disloyalty to the Doctrines of Grace. Published abroad throughout Scotland, it was devoured in the homes of those who belonged to the Praying Societies—men and women who had left the Church of the Revolution Settlement for similar reasons, and were doing their best, without stated ministries, to maintain Christian fellowship in groups that had framed a common rule and were linked in some measure through that rule. They were quite distinct from the Society People to whom John MacMillan ministered. But contacts were frequent, and many members of the Praying Societies had been impressed with the reports from members of the MacMillanite groups of the great spiritual benefit they had personally received from one or other of the solemn assemblies for the renewing of the Covenants ; and since most of the congregations of the Secession had arisen out of these Praying Societies and from their application, either singly or in association, for supply of sermon, it was almost inevitable that they should begin to demand some equivalent in their corporate religious life. The Associate Presbytery was asked to take these requests into consideration. After many discussions, public and private, there emerged in 1743, an *Act of the Associate Presbytery, for Renewing the National Covenant of Scotland, and the Solemn League and Covenant of the three nations, in A WAY and MANNER agreeable to our present SITUATION and CIRCUM-STANCES in this period*. The impression derived from the title, and from the fact that it incorporates the text of the two Covenants, is that here is essentially a repetition of the Cameronian ceremonial, with prob-ably some slight amendments. But the first pages of the lengthy document speedily dispel this notion. The Presbytery state that they cannot conceive it to be their duty to include the civil aspects of the Covenants, or, as they put it, ' to blend civil and ecclesiastical matters in the Oath of God, in renewing the Covenants'; and go on to this explicit statement ' the Presbytery do hereby condemn the *dangerous extreme* that some have gone into, of impugning the present civil author-ity over these Nations, and subjection thereunto in *lawful* commands, on account of the want of these qualifications, which magistrates ought to have by the Word of God and our Covenants ; even though they allow us the free exercise of our religion, and are not manifestly unhinging the Liberties of the Kingdom.' This is evidently the prelude to something more specifically and exclusively religious than the earlier form. And when we read further that, in the process of preparing it, they shed one of their scanty number, who stood for the Cameronian form, declaring that unless ' we pronounce and swear the very Covenants, as at first conceived, with variations accommodated to our present Circumstances, I do not think we can be said properly to renew the Covenants but rather to take a quite different *oath* or *Covenant*,' it becomes apparent that there must be a marked distinction between the two. Both of them print the Covenants, both speak of their continuing, and indeed perpetual, obligation, but while the Cameronians more logically demand, in consequence, that they be renewed with minor adaptations, the Seceders hold that loyalty to their forefathers only demands a form of Covenant in harmony with their high resolves, and incorporating what they take to have been their fundamental religious principles. They conclude their review of the previous history of Christ's Kirk and cause in Scotland with these words : ' Therefore, in obedience to the Command of God, *conform to the practice* of the Godly in former times, and according to the laudable example of our worthy and religious progenitors in the foresaid Covenants.' Then follows the Bond.

We all and every one of us, though sensible of the Deceitfulness and Unbelief of our own Hearts, and however frequently perplexed with Doubts and Fears anent our actual Believing ; yet, desiring to essay, in the Lord's Strength, and in Obedience to his Command, to glorify God, by believing his Word of Grace contained in his Covenant of Promise, and, in the Faith of his Promise, to devote ourselves unto the Lord, in a Covenant of Duty ; We do, with our Hands lifted up to the MOST HIGH GOD, hereby profess, and, before God, Angels and Men, solemnly declare, That, through the Grace of God, and according to the Measure of his Grace given unto us, We do, with our whole Hearts, take hold of the LORD JESUS CHRIST, as the only Propitiation for our Sins ; his *Righteousness*, as the only Foundation of our Accesse to, and Acceptance with God ; his *Covenant* of free and rich Promises, as our only Charter for the heavenly Inheritance ; his *Word* for our perfect and only Rule of Faith and Practice ; his SPIRIT for our alone Guide, to lead us into all Truth revealed in his holy Word, unto which nothing at any time is to be added, whether by new Revelations of the Spirit, or Traditions of Men. We avouch the LORD to be OUR GOD, and in the Strength of his promised Grace, we *promise and swear*, by the GREAT NAME OF THE LORD OUR GOD, That we shall walk in his Way, keep his Judgments and Commandments, and hearken to his Voice ; and, particularly, that we shall, by the Lord's Grace, continue and abide in the Profession, Faith and Obedience of the foresaid true reformed Religion, in Doctrine, Worship, Presbyterial Church-Government and Discipline ; and that we shall, according to our several Stations, Places and Callings, contend and testifie against all contrary Evils, Errors and Corruptions ; particularly, *Popery, Prelacy, Deism, Arrianism, Arminianism*, and every Error subversive of the Doctrine of Grace ; as also *Independency, Latitudinarian-Tenets*, and the other Evils named in the above Confession of Sins.

In like manner, we *promise and swear*, That, by all Means which are lawful and warrantable for us, according to the Word of God, the approven and received Standards of this Church, and our known Principles, we shall, in our several Stations and Callings, endeavour the Reformation of Religion in *England* and *Ireland*, in Doctrine, Worship, Discipline and Government, according to the Word of God ; and to promote and advance our covenanted Conjunction and Uniformity in Religion, Confession of Faith, and Catechisms, Form of Church-Government, and Directory of Worship, as these were received by this Church.

And, in regard we are taught by the Word of God, and

bound by our Covenants, National and Solemn League, to live together in the Fear of God, and in Love one to another, and to encourage one another in the Work and Cause of the Lord ; and that, denying all Ungodliness and worldly Lusts, we should live soberly, righteously and godly in this present World. Therefore, in a Dependence on the Lord's Grace and Strength, we, in the same manner, do *promise* and *swear*, that we shall, in our several Places and Callings, encourage and strengthen one another's Hands, in pursuing the End and Design of this our solemne Oath and Covenant ; and that we shall endeavour a Life and Conversation becoming the Gospel of Christ, and that, in our personal Callings and particular Families, we shall study to be good Examples to one another of Godliness and Righteousness, and of every Duty that we owe to God and Man ; and that we shall not give up ourselves to a detestable Indifference and Neutrality in the Cause of God ; but, denying ourselves, and our own Things, we shall, above all things, seek the Honour of God, and the Good of his Cause and People ; and that, through Grace, forsaking the Counsels of Flesh and Blood, and not leaning upon carnal Confidences, we shall endeavour to depend upon the Lord, to walk by the Rule of his Word, and to hearken to his Voice by his Servants. In all which, professing our own Weakness, we earnestly pray to God, who is the Father of Mercies, through his Son Jesus Christ, to be merciful unto us, and to enable us, by the Power of his HOLY SPIRIT, that we may do our Duty, unto the Praise of his Grace in the Churches. *Amen.*

We might be tempted to give this the credit of being something quite unprecedented in the Church History of our land, were it not for one thing. It is generically distinct from what was done at Auchensaugh, though its final words are a manifest echo of that earlier

Bond, and still more from the national commitments of 1638 and 1643, but it does specifically *claim*, along with many in the history of Israel, one *Scottish* precedent. In the year 1596, at the meeting of the General Assembly in Edinburgh, the first step was taken in what was to prove a general revival of religion throughout the land. Conscious of the slow progress of evangelical truth, the members were led to inquire into the retarding influences. They decided to begin with themselves, to inquire what was lacking in their discharge of their ministerial office, and in their own private conduct and personal religion. A paper cataloguing these shortcomings was drawn up by certain brethren, and suggestions were made for disciplinary dealing with the worst offenders. But the paper proved so heart-searching to the majority of the members that a private session for an exercise of humiliation was demanded. This, conducted by John Davidson of Prestonpans (who was not the Assembly's first choice), was to prove an unforgettable experience in the lives of most who were present. At the end, the Assembly was ready, nay eager, for some definite action. It might simply have renewed the King's Confession of fifteen years before—which was to be the basis of the National Covenant later. But that was not individual enough for the needs of the moment. So, with a keen sense of the mood of the Assembly, the Moderator desired the members to hold up their hands ' to testify their entering into a new league with God.' Men, says David Calderwood, ' were wonderfully moved at the sight of so many hands so readily holden up.' At the next open Session of the Assembly, the following resolution was passed

84

unanimously: 'Forasmuch as the brethren of the Ministry convened in this General Assembly, have, with a solemn humiliation, acknowledged this day their sins, and negligences in their consciences, before God, and have entered into a new covenant with him, protesting to walk more warily in their ways, and more diligently in their charges ; and seeing a great part of the Ministry is not present at this action, the Assembly commandeth the brethren of the synodal Assemblies to make the like solemne humiliation and protestation as was observed by the General, at their next convening ; and so many as be not at the Synod to do it at their Presbytery.' This was duly done ; and in this way the fresh out-pouring of the Spirit, for such the brethren felt it to be, was through the new covenant, transmitted to every Parish in the realm.

That this was the model followed by the Seceders is evident from the steps that they took to put the Act into operation. Nominally a renewal of the Covenants, it was really a solemn act of rededication. A special meeting of the Presbytery was called for Stirling in December 1743. There, the greater part of a day was spent in devotional exercises based mainly on a pre-pared ' Confession of the Sins of the Ministry.' This is, apart from one unfortunate reference to the sin of their countenancing for a time the work of George Whitefield in Scotland, an altogether worthy and soul-searching document, with its repeated ' We desire to be humbled before the Lord ' for this and that negligence and shortcoming in public and in private —in the presentation of the Gospel, in the adminis-tration of the Sacraments, in Pastoral work, in cate-chising, in ecclesiastical administration. Once only does the eagle eye of reproach discern matter for humiliation in a wider context than Scotland. ' We desire to be humbled . . . that we have not duly laid to heart the decayed state of religion in all the Churches of the Reformation and the heavy sufferings of the small remnant in France and other places, who desire to cleave to the Lord ; that we have not been suitably concerned for the Enlargement of Christ's Kingdom, by the downfall of Antichrist and Mahomet, and the in-bringing of the Jews, with the fulness of the Gentiles.' On the second day, after devotional exercises and a relevant sermon, the ancient Covenants and the new Acknowledgement of Sins were read, and then the fifteen ministers present, with uplifted hands, signified their adherence to the New Bond, and finally appended their signatures to it. A second similar meeting at Falkirk in March enrolled the five remaining ministers. Every minister of the Secession Church was now covenanted. The influence was speedily felt in all the scattered congregations, and most of their keenest members pressed forward for a share in the experience. It was 1596 over again, on a smaller scale.

The great success of the movement led the Seceders to take a further step, which was to be the source of considerable controversy later. They laid it down that renewal of the Covenants after the Stirling fashion was to be a term of ministerial communion, exacted even from students entering on their course of study. This was later postponed, after considerable debate, till the time when the student was ready for license. They went on to make it a term of Christian communion, and while this does not seem to have been generally or even widely enforced, it led to bitter local controversies, especially where a minister, fencing the tables and emphasizing the old Covenants rather than the new Bond, seemed to bar the way to scrupulous souls, who felt that approval of the old Covenants carried with it approval of all the seventeenth-century's unspiritual ways of enforcement. Judging from the many pamphlets that survive, it was the suggestion that it was legitimate to seek the ' Extirpation of Prelacy ' by any other means than inducing the deluded to change their views through convincing them by the Word of God, that gave the greatest offence. That is to say, the real stumbling block in the Secession practice as it concerned Church members was that the new Bond masqueraded under an old name.

It is hard to trace the history of its observance among the ministers of the Church. It appears, however, that after the Breach of 1747, the Burghers left it unused ; but among the Anti-burghers it continued as an accepted preliminary in the admission of ministers. For those aspiring to be licentiates, place and date seem to have been named regularly for what was called at times ' renewing the Covenants,' and at times ' taking the Bond.' Normally the observance, conducted by an approved panel of ministers in some convenient centre, lasted for more than one day. Devotional exercises, sermons, and reading of the whole documents, led up to the central act, of which we have more than one trustworthy description, for example : 'The Act of covenanting was performed by the covenanters . . . rising from their seats, and, during the reading of the Bond, holding up their right hands, in token of their solemn engagement to duty by promise and oath. They then subscribed the Bond. . . .' It was this solemn dedication, and the preparation for it, that seems to have been a landmark in many useful lives. And its effect acquired a wider range from the custom, at the close, of asking those who were present and had already taken the Bond, to declare their adherence afresh to their former deed. Without a shadow of doubt this was one of the main instruments in promoting Secession piety.

These, then, are *two* distinct forms taken by the Renewal of the Covenants. But there is a *third* form so closely related that it must be considered along with them. When the Evangelicals who remained within the Church of Scotland saw the success of their former associates in their state of separation, and realized that one source of it was the vigour of their witness against the defections of the times and their posing as the true successors of the heroes of the Second Reformation, it seems to have been brought home to them that it would not be politic to allow the Seceders to monopolize before the nation the rôle of faithful witnesses. Something must be done, they felt, to stem the tide of Secession. A group of them, therefore, met and commissioned John Willison of Dundee, their foremost man in zeal, if not in controversial equipment, to prepare a corresponding document. While doubting of his fitness, he essayed the task, ' hoping to see a witnessing body appear within this Church, as well as without it.' The result was the appearance in 1744 of 'A Fair and Impartial Testimony, essayed in name of a number of Ministers, Elders, and Christian people of the Church of Scotland, unto the laudable Principles, Wrestlings, and Attainments of that Church, and against the Backsliding, Corruptions, Divisions, and

prevailing Evils, both of former and present times.'
This is generally regarded as a counterblast to the
Seceders' *Testimonies*. But on the very title-page
appears, *Attested and Adhered unto by sundry Ministers*—
which makes it an equivalent of the Seceders' *Bond*.

In the catalogue of defections in the Church with
which the Testimony begins, these are viewed, in the
same light, as unfaithfulnesses to the great Covenants
of the past. The point of view is much the same even
to the inclusion of the abolition of the laws against
witchcraft as a symptom of national apostasy. But it
contains in addition some outspoken criticism of the
Fathers of the Secession, *e.g.* ' They ought to have
remembered that the Laws both of God and Man do
highly resent Children's Beating, Cursing or Maltreat-
ing their Mother, even when she is somewhat severe,
and out of her Duty to them : and that it is necessary
that Zeal should be attended with Meekness, Courteous-
ness, and Humbleness of Mind.' In a postscript Mr.
Willison says, ' I doubt not that some may quarrel
me and this *Testimony*, for making too free with the
Associate Brethren ; But they may see I have been
as plain and free with others, and even with the
Established Church relating to Things I judge wrong ;
and this seemed to be necessary to render the *Testimony* the more impartial.' Apart from this candid
appraisement of the action of the Seceders, its whole
tone is much the same. The same sins national and
private are deplored, lamented, bewailed, and testi-
fied against. And the whole document closes with
what is called not an Engagement nor a Bond, but an
Adherence. Here are its terms. ' We, whose Names
are underwritten, having seen and considered the

above paper, called, *A Fair and Impartial Testimony*, etc., do hereby declare, That we think the scope and intention of it good, and that it doth express the Sentiments of many Ministers, Elders, and Christian People of the Church of Scotland, concerning the Principles, Wrestlings and Attainments of the said Church, and concerning the Defections, Corruptions, and Evils therein mentioned. And in regard the said Testimony seems to be drawn up with Impartiality, Plainness, and Uprightness of Design, not to be the Badge of a Party, or a Term of Communion; but a Banner for Truth, a Prompter to Reformation, and the Means of healing Breaches: we humbly judge it needful and seasonable in this day of Backsliding and Division; hoping it may be useful for maintaining and preserving Truth, Purity, and Godliness in the present Age, and for transmitting the same to Posterity; and that it will be either some Check to the Progress of Corruption, or a standing Witness against it. Wherefore we join with the said Testimony in witnessing for the Truths and against the Evils therein specified; and in pleading with our Mother to exert herself to stop Defection, and essay Reformation. And have subscribed these Presents.' Then follow the signatures of eight ministers and two elders, mainly in the Dundee district, representing the group who commissioned it, and who saw it before publication. There is abundant evidence as to the effectiveness of this document in preventing a wholesale landslide into the Secession. That similar complaints to theirs could be voiced within the Church, reconciled many to bear the ills they had. But there is little evidence as to the numbers who subscribed their names. A Secession pamphlet of 1819 has this belittling reference: 'There was one Synod belonging to the Church of Scotland which made an attempt to restore the practice ; but it was an expiring struggle.' Yet there is one indication that it attracted a goodly company. As late as 1765 there was a reissue to about 400 elders and members in the south-west of Scotland who had given in their names as subscribers to the issue, some of them for as many as forty-eight copies. It may therefore be concluded that it did serve its primary purpose, of keeping alive the Evangelical cause within the Church of Scotland, and of depriving the outsiders of the honour of being the sole representatives of banded piety in Scotland.

The subsequent history of the three forms has its own interest. The Church of Scotland form certainly did not outlive the eighteenth century. Indeed, fairly early in the nineteenth century all memory of it seems to have been lost. So entirely, that during the Assembly debate in 1838 on the return of one branch of the Seceders, Dr. Cook could say, ' As to the views of the Associate Synod of the Covenant and the renewing of it as they propose, if that subject be introduced into the General Assembly, he would have to take his leave of the Church of Scotland, and ten thousand besides him would do so. He was quite ready to make great allowance for our forefathers, but we were now a *tolerant* Church.' No Evangelical rose from his seat to remind him of John Willison. That venture of his had already disappeared as a landmark in their past.

The Reformed Presbyterian form of renewal was the one with the longest life. Until the split of 1863 it was a term of Communion. All Reformed Presbyterians were covenanters after the pattern of Auchensaugh. And even when the majority united with the Free Church in 1876, the latter had to give fresh assurance of its loyalty to the Covenants before the Union could take place.

The Secession form had a more interesting and a more troubled history. Within the eighteenth century some ministers had begun to stress what they called the 'descending federal obligation' of the original Covenants, while others had begun to revolt against the Bond itself, just because it seemed—despite its unimpeachable content—to be based on such a descending obligation. Early in the nineteenth century a movement began to make it clear that subscription to the Bond did not imply any such recognition. The protagonist was Dr. Hugh Heugh. He was convinced that many were led through their covenanting to regard themselves as committed to the ancient Covenants in too unqualified a form. The paragraph in the original Acknowledgement of Sins which catalogued as one of the defections of the Church of Scotland the failure of the Assembly of 1690 to assert *the Obligation of our Covenants*, was, he held, responsible for this mistaken attitude. He wanted the reference deleted. For seven years (1810–17) the matter was intermittently before the General Associate Synod. Dr. Heugh had hardly won his point of dissociating the new Covenant from the old ones, when the negotiations for union with the Associate Synod began. The fifth Article of the Basis of Union dealt with this subject, and ran thus : ' We cherish an unfeigned veneration for our Reforming Ancestors, and a deep sense of the inestimable value of the benefits which accrue to us from their noble and successful efforts in the cause of civil and religious liberty ; we approve of the mode adopted by them for mutual excitement and encouragement by solemn confederation and vows to God ; we acknowledge that we are under the strongest obligations, from the efforts which they made, and the privileges which they have transmitted to us, to be grateful to God for what He did by them, and to maintain and prosecute the work of Reformation begun, and, to a great extent, carried on by them : And we assert that Public Religious Vowing or Covenanting is a moral duty to be practised *when the circumstances of Providence require it,* but we agree that the performing or not performing of it shall not be a term of communion.' From the moment when it thus became permissive instead of compulsory, the habit began to disappear ; there seems indeed to be no more than one solitary instance of the public continuance of the practice after 1820, though many good men like Professor Alexander Duncan lamented its disappearance. He claimed that it had secured a higher level in the performance of ministerial duty than would have been possible without it.

Though then discontinued, it did not cease to influence Secession piety. In 1743 there had been a lithographed copy of the original Bond which was widely scattered in Secession homes. It is so like an original document that it is still frequently taken for such. At least five times in the last twenty years I have met families who promised to show me a unique treasure, and have then produced one of these facsimiles. And I have heard more than one say of a ministerial father that he was accustomed to read the Bond on every anniversary of his ordination, and to subject himself to close self-scrutiny in the light of its requirements. It must have made many a solitary worker attempt the little extra which makes so great a difference.

One further influence it had, I believe, in the direction of the missionary efforts of the Seceders. They were specially active in England and in Ireland. And there are many hints in Synod speeches and in pamphlets that one of their main inducements was to reach the goal of the Solemn League and Covenant of an ecclesiastical uniformity in the three Kingdoms through zeal in the preaching of the Word, and to extirpate Prelacy by no civil means, but by unflagging spiritual propaganda. Enlightenment as to legitimate means had not obscured the end their fathers had in view ; and the Presbyterian Churches in England and Ireland owe not a little of their strength and stability to the Seceders' Bond.

APPENDIX

THE NATIONAL COVENANT

WE ALL, and every one of Us underwritten, Protest, that, after long and due Examination of our owne Consciences, in matters of true & false Religion, We are now throughly resolved of the Truth, by the Word and Spirit of God ; and therefore we believe with our hearts, confess with our mouths, subscribe with our hands, and constantly affirme before God, and the whole World, that this onely is the true Christian Faith and Religion, pleasing God, and bringing Salvation to man, which now is by the mercy of God revealed to the world, by the preaching of the blessed Evangel, and receaved, believed, and defended, by many and sundry notable Kirks and Realmes, but chiefly by the *Kirk of Scotland, the Kings Majesty, and three estates of this Realme*, as Gods eternall Truth, and onely ground of our Salvation : as more particularly is expressed in the Confession of our Faith, stablished, and publickly confirmed by sundry Acts of Parliament, and now of a long time hath beene openly professed by the Kings Majesty, and whole body of this Realme both in Burgh and Land. To the which Confession and forme of Religion, wee willingly agree in our consciences in all points, as unto Gods undoubted Truth and Verity, grounded onely upon his written Word. And therefore, we abhorre and detest all contrary Religion, and Doctrine : But chiefly, all kinde of Papistry, in generall and particular heads, even as they are now damned and confuted by the *Word of God, and Kirk of Scotland* : but in special we detest and refuse the usurped authority of that Roman Antichrist upon the Scriptures of God, upon the Kirk, the civill Magistrate, and conscience of men, All his tyrannous lawes made upon indifferent things against our Christian liberty, His erronious Doctrine, against the sufficiency of the written Word, the perfection of the Law, the office of Christ, and his blessed Evangel. His corrupted Doctrine concerning originall sinne, our naturall inability and rebellion to Gods Law, our Justification by faith only, our imperfect Sanctification and obedience to the Law, the nature, number and use of the Holy Sacraments. His five bastard Sacraments, with all his Rites, Ceremonies, and false Doctrine, added to the ministration of the true Sacraments without the Word of God. His cruell judgement against Infants departing without the Sacrament : his absolute necessity of Baptisme : his blasphemous opinion of Transubstantiation, or reall presence of Christs body in the Elements, and receiving of the same by the wicked, or bodies of men. His dispensations with solemne Oathes, Perjuries, and degrees of Mariage forbidden in the Word : his cruelty against the innocent divorced : his divellish Masse : his blasphemous Priesthood : his profane Sacrifice for the sinnes of the dead and the quick : his Canonization of men, calling upon Angels or Saints departed, worshipping of Imagery, Relicts, and Crosses, dedicating of Kirks, Altars, Dayes, Vowes to creatures ; his Purgatory, Prayers for the dead, praying or speaking in a strange language, with his Processions and blasphemous Letany, and multitude of Advocates or Mediators : his manifold Orders, Auricular Confession : his desperate and uncertaine Repentance ; his general and doubtsome Faith ; his satisfactions of men for their sinnes : his Justification by works, *opus operatum*, works of Supererogation, Merits, Pardons, Peregrinations, and Stations : his holy water, baptising of Bells, conjuring of Spirits, crossing, saning, anointing, conjuring, hallowing of *GODS* good creatures, with the superstitious opinion joyned therewith : his Worldly Monarchy, and wicked Hierarchy : his three solemne vowes, with all his shavelings of sundry sorts, his erronious and bloudy decrees made at *Trent*, with all the subscribers and approvers of that cruell and bloudy Band, conjured against the Kirk of *GOD* : and finally, wee detest all his vaine Allegories, Rites, Signes and Traditions, brought in the Kirk, without or against the Word of *GOD*, and Doctrine of this true reformed Kirk, to the which we joyne our selves willingly, in Doctrine, Faith, Religion, Discipline, and use of the Holy Sacraments, as lively members of the same, in Christ our Head : promising and swearing by the *Great Name of the Lord our GOD*, that we shall continue in the obedience of the Doctrine and Discipline of this Kirk, and shall defend the same according to our vocation and Power, all the dayes of our lives, under the pains contained in the Law, and danger both of Body and Soul, in the day of GODS fearful judgment : And seeing that many are stirred up by Sathan, and that Roman Antichrist, to promise, sweare, subscribe, and for a time use the Holy Sacraments in the Kirk deceitfully against their own Consciences, minding thereby, first, under the external cloak of Religion, to corrupt and subvert secretly GODS true Religion within the Kirk, and afterward, when time may serve, to become open enemies and persecutors of the same, under vain hope of the Popes dispensation, devised against the Word of GOD, to his greater confusion, and their double condemnation in the day of the LORD JESUS.

Wee, therefore, willing to take away all suspicion of hypocrisy, and of such double dealing with GOD and his Kirk, Protest, and call *The Searcher of all hearts* for witnesse, that Our mindes and hearts, do fully agree with this our *Confession, Promise, Oath* and *Subscription*, so that Wee are not moved for any worldly respect, but are persuaded onely in our Consciences, through the knowledge and love of Gods true Religion, printed in our hearts by the Holy Spirit, as we shall answer to him in the day, when the secrets of all hearts shall be disclosed. And because we perceave that the quietness and stability of our Religion and Kirk, doth depend upon the safety & good behaviour of the Kings Majesty, as upon a comfortable Instrument of Gods mercy, granted to this Countrey, for the maintaining of this Kirk, and ministration of Justice amongst us, we protest and promise with our hearts under the same Oath, Hand-writ, and Pains, that we shall defend his Person and Authority, with our goods, bodies and lives, in the defence of Christ his Evangel, Liberties of our Country, ministration of Justice, and punishment of iniquity, against all enemies within this Realm, or without, as we desire our GOD to be a strong and merciful defender to us in the day of our death, and coming of our Lord *Jesus Christ* : To whom with the Father, and the Holy Spirit, be all Honour and Glory Eternally.

Like as many Acts of Parliament not onely in general do abrogate, annull, and rescind all Lawes, Statutes, Acts, Constitutions, Canons, civil or municipall, with all other Ordinances and practique penalties whatsoever, made in prejudice of the true Religion and Professours thereof ; Or, of the true Kirk-discipline, jurisdiction, and freedome thereof; Or in favours of Idolatry and Superstition ; Or of the Papisticall Kirk ; As *Act.* 3. *Act* 13. *Parl.* 1. *Act.* 23. *Parl.* 11. *Act.* 114. *Parl.* 12. of *King Iames the sixt,* That Papistry and Superstition may be utterly suppressed according to the intention of the Acts of Parliament repeated in the 5. *Act. Parl.* 20. *K. Iames* 6. And to that end they ordaine all Papists and Priests to be punished by manifold Civill and Ecclesiastical pains, as adversaries to Gods true Religion, preached and by Law established within this Realme, *Act.* 24. *Parl.* 11. *K. Iames* 6. as common enemies to all Christian government, *Act.* 18. *Parl.* 16. *K. Iames* 6. as rebellers and gainstanders of our Soveraigne Lords Authority, *Act.* 47. *Parl.* 3. *K. Iames* 6. and as Idolaters. *Act.* 104. *Parl.* 7. *K. Iames* 6. but also in particular (by and attour the Confession of Faith) do abolish and condemne the Popes Authority and Jurisdiction out of this Land, and ordaine the maintainers thereof to be punished, *Act* 2. *Parl.* 1. *Act* 51. *Parl.* 3. *Act* 106. *Parl.* 7. *Act* 114. *Parl.* 12. *K. Iames* 6. do condemne the Popes erronious doctrine, or any other erronious doctrine repugnant to any of the Articles of the true and Christian religion publickly preached, and by law established in this Realme : And ordaines the spreaders and makers of Books or Libels, or Letters, or writs of that nature to be punished, *Act* 46. *Parl.* 3. *Act* 106. *Parl.* 7. *Act* 24.

Parl. 11. *K. Iames* 6. do condemne all Baptisme conforme to the Popes Kirk and the Idolatry of the Masse, and ordaines all sayers, willfull hearers, and concealers of the Masse, the maintainers and resetters of the Priests, Jesuites, traffiquing Papists, to be punished without any exception or restriction, *Act* 5. *Parl.* 1. *Act.* 120. *Parl.* 12. *Act.* 164. *Parl.* 13. *Act.* 193. *Parl.* 14. *Act.* 1. *Parl.* 19. *Act.* 5. *Parl.* 20. *K. Iames* 6. do condemne all erroneous bookes and writtes containing erroneous doctrine against the Religion presently professed, or containing superstitious Rites and Ceremonies Papisticall, whereby the people are greatly abused, and ordaines the home-bringers of them to be punished, *Act* 25. *Parl.* 11. *K. Iames* 6. do condemne the monuments and dregs of by-gone Idolatry ; as going to the Crosses, observing the Feastivall dayes of Saints, and such other superstitious and Papisticall Rites, to the dishonour of GOD, contempt of true Religion, and fostering of great errour among the people, and ordaines the users of them to be punished for the second fault as Idolaters, *Act* 104. *Parl.* 7. *K. Iames* 6.

Like as many Acts of Parliament are conceaved for maintenance of GODS true and Christian Religion, and the purity thereof in Doctrine and Sacraments of the true Church of God, the liberty & freedom thereof, in her National, Synodal Assemblies, Presbyteries, Sessions, Policy, Discipline and Jurisdiction thereof, as that purity of Religion and liberty of the Church was used, professed, exercised, preached and confessed according to the reformation of Religion in this Realm. As for instance, *The* 99. *Act. Parl.* 7. *Act.* 23. *Parl.* 11. *Act.* 114. *Parl.* 12. *Act.* 160. *Parl.* 13. *of King Iames* 6. Ratified by the 4. *Act.* of King *Charles.* So that the 6. *Act. Parl.* 1. and 68. *Act. Parl.* 6. of King *Iames* 6. in the Yeare of God 1579. declares the Ministers of the blessed Evangel, whom GOD of his mercy had raised up, or hereafter should raise, agreeing with them that then lived in Doctrin, and Administration of the Sacraments, and the People that professed Christ, as he was then offered in the Evangel, and doth communicate with the Holy Sacraments, (as in the reformed Kirk's of this Realm they were publickly

administrat) according to the Confession of Faith, to be the
true and Holy Kirk of Christ Jesus within this Realm, and
decerns and declares all and sundry, who either gainsayes
the Word of the Evangel, received and approved, as the
heads of the Confession of Faith, professed in Parliament,
in the Yeare of God 1560. specified also in the first Parliament of King *Iames* 6. and ratified in this present Parliament,
more particularly do specify, or that refuses the administration of the Holy Sacraments, as they were then minis-
trated, to be no members of the said Kirk within this Realme,
and true Religion, presently professed, so long as they keep
themselves so divided from the society of Christs body :
And the subsequent *Act.* 69. *Parl.* 6. of *K. Iames* 6. declares,
That there is none other Face of Kirk, nor other Face of
Religion, then was presently at that time, by the Favour of
GOD established within this Realme, which therefore is
ever stiled, *Gods true Religion, Christs true Religion, the true and
Christian Religion, and a perfect Religion,* Which by manifold
acts of Parliament, all within this realme are bound to
subscribe the articles thereof, the Confession of Faith, to
recant all doctrine & errours, repugnant to any of the said
Articles, *Act.* 4. & 9. *Parl.* 1. *Act.* 45. 46. 47. *Parl.* 3. *Act* 71.
Parl. 6. *Act* 106. *Parl.* 7. *Act* 24. *Parl.* 11. *Act* 123. *Parl.* 12.
Act 194. *and* 197. *Parl.* 14. *of K. Iames* 6. And all Magistrats,
Sherifs, &c. on the one parte are ordained to search, appre-
hend, and punish all contraveeners ; For instance, *Act* 5.
Parl. 1. *Act* 104. *Parl.* 7. *Act* 25. *Parl.* 11. *K. Iames* 6. And that
notwithstanding of the Kings Majesty's licences on the
contrary, which are discharged & declared to be of no force
in so farre as they tend in any wayes, to the prejudice &
hinder of the execution of the Acts of Parliament against
Papists & adversaries of true Religion, *Act.* 106. *Parl.* 7.
K. Iames 6. On the other part in the 47. *Act. Parl.* 3. *K. Iames*
6. It is declared and ordained, seeing the cause of Gods
true Religion, and his highnes Authority are so joyned, as
the hurt of the one is common to both : and that none shal
be reputed as loyall and faithfull subjects to our Soveraigne
Lord, or his Authority, but be punishable as rebellers and

gainstanders of the same, who shall not give their Confession, and make their profession of the said true Religion, and that they who after defection shall give the Confession of their Faith of new, they shall promise to continue therein in time comming, to maintaine our Souveraigne Lords Authority, and at the uttermost of their power to fortify, assist, and maintaine the true Preachers and Professors of Christs Evangel, against whatsoever enemies and gainestanders of the same ; and namely (against all such of whatsoever nation, estate, or degree they be of) that have joyned, and bound themselves, or have assisted, or assists to set forward, and execute the cruell decrees of *Trent*, contrary to the Preachers and true Professors of the Word of God, which is repeated word by word in the Article of Pacification at *Perth* the 23 of Februar. 1572. approved by Parliament the last of Aprile 1573. Ratified in Parliament 1587. and related, *Act* 123. *Parl* 12. *of K. James* 6. with this addition, that they are bound to resist all treasonable uproars and hostilities raised against the true Religion, the Kings Majesty, and the true Professors.

Like as all Lieges are bound to maintaine the King Majesty's Royal Person, and Authority, the Authority of Parliaments, without the which neither any lawes or lawful judicatories can be established, *Act* 130. *Act.* 131. *Parl.* 8. *K. Iames* 6. and the subjects Liberties, who ought onely to live and be governed by the Kings lawes, the common lawes of this Realme allanerly, *Act* 48. *Parl.* 3. *K. Iames the first. Act.* 79. *Parl.* 6. *K. Iames the 4. repeated in the Act* 131. *Parl.* 8. *K. Iames* 6. Which, if they be innovated or prejudged, the commission anent the union of the two Kingdoms of *Scotland* and *England*, which is the sole *Act of the* 17. *Parl. of K. Iames* 6. declares such confusion would ensue, as this Realme could be no more a free Monarchy, because by the fundamentall lawes, ancient priviledges, offices and liberties, of this Kingdome, not onely the Princely Authority of his Majesty's Royal discent hath been these many ages maintained, but also the peoples security of their Lands, livings, rights, offices, liberties, and dignities preserved, and therefore for the preservation of the said true Religion, Lawes, and Liberties of this Kingdome, it is statute by the 8. *Act Parl.* 1. *repeated in the* 99. *Act Parl.* 7. *Ratified in the* 23. *Act Parl.* 11. *and* 114. *Act Parl.* 12. *of K. Iames* 6. *and* 4. *Act of K. Charles.* That all Kings and Princes at their Coronation and reception of their Princely Authority, shall make their faithfull promise by their solemne oath in the presence of the Eternal God, that, enduring the whole time of their lives, they shall serve the same Eternal God to the uttermost of their power, according as he hath required in his most Holy Word, contained in the old and new Testament. And according to the same Word shall maintain the true Religion of Christ Jesus, the preaching of his Holy Word, the due and right ministration of the Sacraments now receaved and preached within this Realme (according to the Confession of Faith immediately preceeding) and shall abolish and gainstand all false Religion contrary to the same, and shall rule the people committed to their charge, according to the will and command of God, revealed in his foresaid Word, and according to the laudable Lawes and Constitutions received in this Realme, no wayes repugnant to the said will of the Eternall God ; and shall procure, to the uttermost of their power, to the Kirk of God, and whole Christian people, true and perfite peace in all time coming : and that they shall be careful to root out of their Empire all Hereticks, and enemies to the true worship of God, who shall be convicted by the true Kirk of God, of the foresaid crimes, which was also observed by his Majesty, at his Coronation in *Edinburgh* 1633. as may be seene in the order of the Coronation.

In obedience to the Commandment of GOD, conforme to the practice of the godly in former times, and according to the laudable example of our Worthy and Religious Progenitors, & of many yet living amongst us, which was warranted also by act of *Councill*, commanding a general band to be made and subscribed by his Majesty's subjects, of all ranks, for two causes : One was, For defending the true Religion, as it was then reformed, and is expressed in the Confession of Faith abovewritten, and a former large

Confession established by sundry acts of lawful generall
assemblies, & of Parliament, unto which it hath relation,
set down in publick Catechismes, and which had been for
many years with a blessing from Heaven preached, and
professed in this Kirk and Kingdome, as Gods undoubted
truth, grounded only upon his written Word. The other
cause was, for maintaining the Kings Majesty, His Person,
and Estate : the true worship of GOD and the Kings
authority, being so straitly joined, as that they had the same
Friends, and common enemies, and did stand and fall
together. And finally, being convinced in our mindes, and
confessing with our mouthes, that the present and succeeding
generations in this Land, are bound to keep the foresaid
nationall Oath & Subscription inviolable, Wee Noblemen,
Barons, Gentlemen, Burgesses, Ministers & Commons
under subscribing, considering divers times before &
especially at this time, the danger of the true reformed
Religion, of the Kings honour, and of the publick peace of
the Kingdome : By the manifold innovations and evills
generally conteined, and particularly mentioned in our late
supplications, complaints, and protestations, Do hereby
professe, and before *God*, his Angels, and the World solemnly
declare, That, with our whole hearts we agree & resolve,
all the dayes of our life, constantly to adhere unto, and to
defend the foresaid true Religion, and (forbearing the
practice of all novations, already introduced in the matters
of the worship of GOD, or approbation of the corruptions
of the publicke Government of the Kirk, or civil places and
power of Kirk-men, till they be tryed & allowed in free
assemblies, and in Parliaments) to labour by all meanes
lawful to recover the purity and liberty of the Gospel, as it
was stablished and professed before the foresaid Novations :
and because, after due examination, we plainely perceave,
and undoubtedly believe, that the Innovations and evils
contained in our Supplications, Complaints, and Protestations have no warrant of the Word of *God*, are contrary to the
Articles of the Foresaid Confessions, to the intention and
meaning of the blessed reformers of Religion in this Land,

to the above written Acts of Parliament, & do sensibly tend to the re-establishing of the Popish Religion and Tyranny, and to the subversion and ruine of the true Reformed Religion, and of our Liberties, Lawes and Estates, We also declare, that the Foresaid Confessions are to be interpreted, and ought to be understood of the Foresaid novations and evils, no lesse then if every one of them had been expressed in the Foresaid confessions, and that we are obliged to detest & abhorre them amongst other particular heads of Papistry abjured therein. And therefore from the knowledge and consciences of our duety to *God*, to our King and Countrey, without any worldly respect or inducement, so farre as humane infirmity will suffer, wishing a further measure of the grace of *God* for this effect, We promise, and sweare by the *Great Name of the Lord our GOD*, to continue in the Profession and Obedience of the Foresaid Religion : That we shall defend the same, and resist all these contrary errours and corruptions, according to our vocation, and to the uttermost of that power that *GOD* hath put in our hands, all the dayes of our life : and in like manner with the same heart, we declare before GOD and Men, That we have no intention nor desire to attempt any thing that may turne to the dishonour of GOD, or to the diminution of the Kings greatnesse and authority : But on the contrary, we promise and sweare, that we shall, to the uttermost of our power, with our meanes and lives, stand to the defence of our dread Soveraigne, the Kings Majesty, his Person, and Authority, in the defence and preservation of the foresaid true Religion, Liberties and Lawes of the Kingdome : As also to the mutual defence and assistance, every one of us of another in the same cause of maintaining the true Religion and his Majesty's Authority, with our best counsel, our bodies, meanes, and whole power, against all sorts of persons whatsoever. So that whatsoever shall be done to the least of us for that cause, shall be taken as done to us all in genearal, and to every one of us in particular. And that we shall neither directly nor indirectly suffer our selves to be divided or withdrawn by whatsoever suggestion, allurement, or terrour from this blessed & loyall Conjunction, nor shall cast in any let or impediment, that may stay or hinder any such resolution as by common consent shall be found to conduce for so good ends. But on the contrary, shall by all lawful meanes labour to further and promove the same, and if any such dangerous & divisive motion be made to us by Word or Writ, We, and every one of us, shall either suppresse it, or if need be shall incontinent make the same known, that it may be timeously obviated : neither do we fear the foul aspersions of rebellion, combination, or what else our adversaries from their craft and malice would put upon us, seing what we do is so well warranted, and ariseth from an unfeined desire to maintaine the true worship of God, the Majesty of our King, and peace of the Kingdome, for the common happinesse of our selves, and the posterity. And because we cannot look for a blessing from God upon our proceedings, except with our Profession and Subscription we joine such a life & conversation, as beseemeth Christians, who have renewed their Covenant with God ; We, therefore, faithfully promise, for our selves, our followers, and all other under us, both in publick, in our particular families, and personal carriage, to endeavour to keep our selves within the bounds of Christian liberty, and to be good examples to others of all Godlinesse, Sobernesse, and Righteousnesse, and of every duety we owe to God and Man, And that this our Union and Conjunction may be observed without violation, we call the living GOD, the Searcher of our Hearts to witness, who knoweth this to be our sincere Desire, and unfained Resolution, as we shall answere to JESUS CHRIST, in the great day, and under the pain of Gods everlasting wrath, and of infamy, and losse of all honour and respect in this World, Most humbly beseeching the Lord to strengthen us by his holy Spirit for this end, and to blesse our desires and proceedings with a happy successe, that Religion and Righteousnesse may flourish in the Land, to the glory of GOD, the honour of King, and peace and comfort of us all. In witnesse whereof we have subscribed with our hands all the premisses, &c.

THE SOLEMN LEAGUE AND COVENANT

We Noblemen, Barons, Knights, Gentlemen, Citizens, Burgesses, Ministers of the Gospel, and Commons of all sorts in the Kingdoms of *Scotland*, *England* and *Ireland*, by the providence of GOD living under one King, and being of one reformed Religion, Having before our eyes the glory of GOD, and the advancement of the Kingdom of our Lord and Saviour Jesus Christ, the Honour and Happinesse of the Kings Majesty and his Posterity, and the true publick Liberty, Safety, and Peace of the Kingdoms, wherein every ones private condition is included ; And calling to minde the treacherous and bloody Plots, conspiracies, Attempts and Practices of the Enemies of GOD against the true Religion and Professours thereof in all places, especially in these three Kingdoms, ever since the Reformation of Religion, and how much their rage, power and presumption are of late, and at this time increased and exercised ; whereof the deplorable estate of the Church and Kingdom of *Ireland*, the distressed estate of the Church & Kingdom of *England*, and the dangerous estate of the Church and Kingdom of *Scotland* are present and publick testimonies : We have now at last (after other means of Supplication, Remonstrance, Protestation and Suffering) for the preservation of our selves and our Religion from utter ruine and destruction, according to the commendable practice of these Kingdoms in former times, and the example of GODS People in other Nations, after mature deliberation, resolved and determined to enter into a mutuall and solemn League and Covenant : Wherein we all subscribe, and each one of us for himself, with our hands lifted up to the most high GOD, do Swear.

1. That we shall sincerely, really and constantly, through the grace of GOD, endeavour in our several places and callings, the preservation of the Reformed Religion in the Church of *Scotland*, in Doctrine, Worship, Discipline and Government, against our common Enemies ; The Reforma-

tion of Religion in the Kingdoms of *England* and *Ireland*, in Doctrine, Worship, Discipline and Government, according to the Word of GOD, and the example of the best Reformed Churches ; And shall endeavour to bring the Churches of GOD in the three Kingdoms, to the nearest conjunction and Uniformity in Religion, Confession of Faith, Form of Church-government, Directory for Worship and Catechizing; That we and our Posterity after us, may, as Brethren, live in Faith and Love, and the Lord may delight to dwell in the midst of us.

2. That we shall in like manner, without respect of persons, endeavour the Extirpation of Popery, Prelacy (that is, Church-government by Arch-bishops, Bishops, their Chancellours and Commissaries, Deans, Deans and Chapters, Arch-deacons, and all other Ecclesiasticall Officers depending on that Hierarchy) Superstition, Heresy, Schism, Prophanesse, and whatsoever shall be found to be contrary to sound Doctrine, and the power of Godliness ; Lest we partake in other mens sins, and thereby be in danger to receive of their plagues ; And that the Lord may be one, and his Name one in the three Kingdoms.

3. We shall with the same sincerity, reality and constancy, in our severall vocations, endeavour with our estates and lives mutually to preserve the Rights and Priviledges of the Parliaments, and the Liberties of the Kingdoms ; And to preserve and defend the Kings Majesty's Person and Authority, in the preservation and defence of the true Religion, and Liberties of the Kingdoms ; That the world may bear witnesse with our consciences of our Loyalty, and that we have no thoughts or intentions to diminish his Majesty's just power and greatnesse.

4. We shall also with all faithfulnesse endeavour the discovery of all such as have been, or shall be Incendiaries, Malignants, or evil instruments, by hindering the Reformation of Religion, dividing the King from his people, or one of the Kingdoms from another, or making any faction, or parties amongst the people contrary to this League and Covenant, That they may be brought to publick triall, and

receive condigne punishment, as the degree of their offences shall require or deserve, or the supream Judicatories of both Kingdomes respectively, or others having power from them for that effect, shall judge convenient.

5. And whereas the happinesse of a blessed Peace between these Kingdoms, denyed in former times to our Progenitors, is by the good Providence of *GOD* granted unto us, and hath been lately concluded, and settled by both Parliaments, We shall each one of us, according to our place and interest, endeavour that they may remain conjoyned in a firme Peace and Union to all Posterity, And that Justice may be done upon the willfull Opposers thereof, in manner expressed in the precedent Article.

6. We shall also according to our places and callings in this Common cause of Religion, Liberty, and Peace of the Kingdoms, assist and defend all those that enter into this League and Covenant, in the maintaining and pursuing thereof ; And shall not suffer our selves directly or indirectly by whatsoever combination, perswasion or terrour, to be divided and withdrawn from this blessed Union and conjunction, whither to make defection to the contrary part, or to give our selves to a detestable indifferency or neutrality in this cause, which so much concerneth the Glory of *GOD*, the good of the Kingdoms, and honour of the King ; But shall all the dayes of our lives zealously and constantly continue therein, against all opposition, and promote the same according to our power, against all Lets and Impediments whatsoever ; And, what we are not able our selves to suppresse or overcome, we shall reveale and make known, that it may be timely prevented or removed : All which we shall do as in the sight of *GOD*..

And because these Kingdoms are guilty of many sins, and provocations against *GOD*, and his Son Jesus Christ, as is too manifest by our present distresses and dangers, the fruits thereof, We professe and declare before *GOD*, and the world, our unfained desire to be humbled for our own sins, and for the sins of these Kingdoms, especially that we have not, as we ought, valued the inesteemable benefit of the Gospel, that we have not laboured for the purity and power thereof, and that we have not endeavoured to receive Christ in our hearts, nor to walk worthy of him in our lives, wich are the causes of other sins and transgressions so much abounding amongst us, And our true and unfained purpose, desire, and endeavour for our selves, and all others under our power and charge, both in publick and in private, in all dutyes we owe to *GOD* and man, to amend our lives, and each one to go before another in the example of a real Reformation ; That the Lord may turn away his wrath, and heavy indignation, and establish these Churches and Kingdoms in truth and Peace. And this Covenant we make in the presence of Almighty *GOD* the Searcher of all hearts, with a true intention to perform the same, As we shall answer at that great Day when the secrets of all hearts, shall be disclosed ; Most humbly beseeching the Lord, to strengthen us by his Holy Spirit for this end, and to blesse our desires, and proceedings with such successe, as may be deliverance and safety to his people, and encouragement to other Christian Churches groaning under, or in danger of the yoke of Antichristian Tyranny, or to joyn in the same, or like Association & Covenant, To the Glory of *GOD*, the enlargement of the Kingdom of Jesus Christ, and the peace & tranquillity of Christian Kingdoms, and Common-wealths.